IMAGES
of America

CAMP WILLIAM PENN

The very popular recruitment poster of Camp William Penn soldiers of the 25th Regiment United States Colored Troops and their officer was widely circulated from mid-1863 through the end of the Civil War in 1865. The depiction appealed to black men wanting to enlist in the Civil War. The words "Rally Round the Flag, boys! Rally once again, Shouting the battle cry of FREEDOM!" were central to the equality messages of antislavery abolitionists. The color lithograph, engraved by P. S. Duval and Son in Philadelphia, was developed from an earlier black-and-white photograph (on the cover) of the Camp William Penn warriors. (Library Company of Philadelphia.)

On the cover: Please see page 26. (Dr. James Spina.)

IMAGES
of America

CAMP WILLIAM PENN

Donald Scott Sr.

ARCADIA
PUBLISHING

ISBN 978-0-7385-5735-9

Published by Arcadia Publishing
Charleston, South Carolina

Printed in the United States of America

Library of Congress Catalog Card Number: 2007937574

For all general information contact Arcadia Publishing at:
Telephone 843-853-2070
Fax 843-853-0044
E-mail sales@arcadiapublishing.com
For customer service and orders:
Toll-Free 1-888-313-2665

Visit us on the Internet at www.arcadiapublishing.com

To my wife Billie, who shared my vision with love, and my parents, Dr. Henry Scott and Mrs. Grace Scott, brothers, sons, family, and friends for their immense support

Contents

Acknowledgments

This project would not have been possible without information from numerous supporters, government agencies, historical organizations, institutions, and the personal collections of the soldiers' descendants.

Offered through the professional courtesies of committed staff at the National Archives, Library of Congress, U.S. Army Military History Institute, New Jersey State Archives, and National Park Service were countless treasures.

Further information obtained came from the Citizens for the Restoration of Historic LaMott (CROHL); Historical Society of Pennsylvania; Gilder Lehrman Collection at the New York Historical Society, Gilder Lehrman Institute of American History; Old York Road Historical Society, Cheltenham; Virginia Historical Society, Richmond, Virginia; Cheltenham Historical Commission; Adams County Historical Society, Gettysburg, Pennsylvania; Abraham Lincoln Foundation Board, Union League of Philadelphia; and the Library Company of Philadelphia.

The Free Library of Philadelphia; Schomburg Center for Research in Black Culture, New York Public Library; Civil War and Underground Railroad Museum, Philadelphia; GAR Civil War Museum, Philadelphia; St. Paul's Episcopal Church, Elkins Park; Mother Bethel African Methodist Episcopal Church, Philadelphia; African American Civil War Museum and Memorial, Washington, D.C.; University of Pennsylvania; Bryn Mawr College Collections, gift of Joseph M. Fox; Friends Historical Library at Swarthmore College; and Virginia Foundation for the Humanities provided contributions of significance.

My gratitude for the personal collections or references extended by Donald McMurray, Lee Carol Cook, William A. Gladstone, the late Perry Triplett, Norman Triplett, James Spina, Joyce Werkman, Thomas I. Dawson, Cicero Green, Lise Marlowe, Bill Chambrés, Jacinta and Donald Scott Jr., Bonnie and Kristopher Scott, and 3rd Regiment USCT Re-enactors, Philadelphia.

My sincerest appreciation for the invaluable consultation offered by respected Virginia scholars Jerome S. Handler and Michael L. Tuite Jr.; prominent local historians Andy Waskie, James M. Paradis, Leroy Hopkins, Eric Ledell Smith, David Rowland, Bruce Mowday, Rev. Dr. Jeffrey Leath, and James Elton Johnson; and the knowledge shared by recognized authorities on black military history, author Robert Greene and my father-in-law, Lt. Comdr. Wesley A. Brown, retired, the first black graduate of U.S. Naval Academy, 1949.

Finally, this book gives the highest honors to the warriors of Camp William Penn who gave so much for our liberty.

INTRODUCTION

The story of Camp William Penn, the first and largest federal facility to train Northern-based black soldiers during the Civil War, is the quintessential American saga. Although tragically forgotten in most U.S. history books, there is barely an American photographic narrative that compares to the depth and importance of eastern Pennsylvania's Camp William Penn, erected during the summer of 1863 as the Civil War raged and the Union army celebrated one of its first major victories at Gettysburg.

The camp and its surrounding Chelten Hills community became an unparalleled epicenter in the fight for women's rights, and particularly, for black liberty, as the Confederate army began to threaten the heart of the Union—Washington, D.C., and Philadelphia. Pres. Abraham Lincoln became convinced that in order to save the Union, it was imperative for him to recruit black federal troops. That decision, spurred by antislavery abolitionists, launched a massive movement for black rights—most notably by the black soldiers who enlisted in hope that they would prove themselves equal to whites and worthy of liberty, as well as suffrage.

As the country convulsed due to its life-threatening illness, slavery, some of America's most acclaimed photographers, and others less well known, began to record just about every aspect of the debacle—from the horrors of slavery and lynching of blacks to the abhorrent Civil War prison camps. They recorded battle scenes and hospitals where many of the wounded were in even more trouble due to unsanitary conditions and archaic surgical techniques. Indeed, rare and very valuable photographs of Camp William Penn soldiers were also shot, as well as depictions of the battles in which the black soldiers from the camp fought. Such recorded images included the famous antislavery abolitionists, as well as top generals, officers, and most important for this project, the black recruits. There are thousands of photographed service records of the men, as well as numerous recruiting broadsides or advertisements that appeared on city streets and town halls, urging new recruits to join the fight to save the country and stomp out slavery.

After all, Camp William Penn's black soldiers fought in many of the major battles of the Civil War from 1863 through 1865, just as photographic and illustrative evidence indicates. They pursued Pres. Abraham Lincoln's assassins and led his funeral, as well as cornered Gen. Robert E. Lee and his army before witnessing the Southerners' surrender. They were among the first troops to enter the burning Confederate capital of Richmond. Several, in fact, earned the prestigious Medal of Honor for heroic and meritorious deeds during the war. They were among more than 180,000 black warriors who fought in the Civil War and today are honored in Washington, D.C., with their names engraved on the African American Civil War Memorial.

Although some have doubted if a book displaying about 200 images concerning Camp William Penn could ever be produced, I sensed that because of the sheer number of soldiers who trained there, consisting of 11 regiments with about 1,000 recruits each, such material had to be available. I would have to cast a very wide net. My wife Billie and I scoured repositories in Pennsylvania; New Jersey; Maryland; Virginia; Washington, D.C.; and New York. Via the Web, I contacted research or historical facilities in such states as Ohio, Texas, and Michigan Over the past six months, I had minimally sent out 500 e-mail inquiries. The search had been grueling, long, but exceptionally rewarding—especially when we would find the elderly ebony face of a soldier who had been all but forgotten in time, but who served and saved America after being trained at Camp William Penn. And in the process, such men knocked out many of the racist stereotypes of the day that labeled African American soldiers as cowards, ignorant and incompetent.

Yet our research confirmed that many of those forgotten warriors were scorned even after the war due to persistent racism, often finding it extremely difficult to obtain government pensions for themselves, wives, and children. Photographic images of their families, letters, and other documents reflect this sad reality.

Still there were also images of great notoriety. Not only did the camp, situated just several miles northwest of Philadelphia, attract almost 11,000 ex-slaves, free blacks, and white officers to "strike the blow" for liberty and repel the rebels, it drew in such famous abolitionists as orator Frederick Douglass; the Underground Railroad's supreme conductor Harriet Tubman; the "father of the Underground Railroad," William Still; as well as the "most revered woman in America," Lucretia Mott, whose Roadside estate sat adjacent to Camp William Penn. Mott, the preeminent women's rights advocate, was also one of the most fierce antislavery proponents in the country, meeting at her home with the above individuals, as well as the great poet and writer John Greenleaf Whittier, journalist and editor William Lloyd Garrison, and activist and author Wendell Oliver Holmes. Regarding women's rights, Mott met at Roadside with the great Elizabeth Cady Stanton and Susan B. Anthony.

Furthermore, just a stone's throw from the camp rested the home of Jay Cooke, "the financier of the Civil War," who entertained the victorious Union general at his Ogontz estate—Pres. Ulysses S. Grant, whose son Jesse attended a private military academy in the area following the war. It was Cooke's grand mansion that set the tone for the neighborhood as the Gilded Age of the late 1800s and early 1900s zoomed in, attracting to the neighborhood the famous hatmaker John B. Stetson, department store magnate John Wannamaker, transportation tycoons and partners Peter A. B. Widener and William Elkins, ice-cream mogul Henry W. Breyers, and many others. All of those wealthy folks built grand mansions near where the black troops—many of them tattered and enslaved just before arriving at Camp William Penn—would train for the fight of their lives on the battlefield and in American society.

Yet in 1859, when Peter A. B. Widener began to build his great wealth, starting as a simple butcher who began to serve the Union army in Philadelphia, a woman named Mary Brown, in the throes of depression, sought refuge in the Roadside home of Lucretia Mott. The Quaker abolitionist readily opened her doors to her, whose husband, John Brown, began his march to the gallows for his unsuccessful raid on Harper's Ferry. Mary Brown had even penned a letter to her children, trying to comfort them about their father's impending execution. In the midst of that despair, John Brown—a white abolitionist—made a hair-raising prediction: that the country would erupt into a great and bloody civil war due to the perpetuation of slavery.

As 1861 approached and the Civil War became eminent, Mott's son-in-law Edward M. Davis served as an officer in the Union army under a liberal associate of his mother-in-law. His name was Gen. John C. Fremont, one of the first Union officers to push for the abolition of slavery and the recruitment of black soldiers. But, due to political considerations, Lincoln refused to move immediately forward on those issues for fear of offending border states that might drift to the side of the sulking Confederacy. Some historians, in fact, speculate that Abraham Lincoln's Emancipation Proclamation of January 1, 1863, was actually patterned off of the original decree of Fremont, who himself would unsuccessfully run for president.

Ultimately, the 1863 Confederate invasion of Pennsylvania and that southern army's move into Gettysburg changed Lincoln's mind and the course of American history. On May 22, 1863, the U.S. War Department issued General Order 143 that established the Bureau of Colored Troops. The Supervisory Committee to Recruit Officers for Negro Troops was established at 1210 Chestnut Street in Philadelphia, supported by such army officers as Maj. George L. Stearns, Maj. Gen. Benjamin F. Butler, Col. John H. Taggart, and Col. Thomas Wentworth Higginson, a "secret" supporter of the antislavery abolitionist John Brown.

Once returning home to Philadelphia, Edward M. Davis joined a new club of privileged white men dedicated to upholding the principles of Lincoln and keeping the Union. It would be called the Union League of Philadelphia, an organization that immediately started raising money for Union causes and would soon contribute handily to financing the establishment of Camp William Penn.

The black soldiers at Camp William Penn would soon march off to war and routinely salute the little gray-haired Quaker woman, Lucretia Mott, standing or sitting on her porch. They generally adored her freshly baked pies and outspokenness for their equality and bravery. They greatly respected Mott joining hands with the likes of the majestic Frederick Douglass, who spoke to the new recruits of the 3rd Regiment United States Colored Troops (USCT). It was the first regiment to leave Camp William Penn later that summer, although local white authorities refused to let the black men parade through Philadelphia with guns for fear they would incite a riot by those fearing African American retribution for racism and slavery.

After leaving the city, and led by Col. Benjamin C. Tilghman, the 3rd Regiment USCT would participate in the siege of Fort Wagner in South Carolina where the Massachusetts 54th valiantly fought earlier, as depicted in the motion picture *Glory*. It would also see action during early 1864 in Florida at the bloody Battle of Olustee, depicted in several images, and where the 8th Regiment USCT of Camp William Penn suffered very heavy casualties after being ambushed by veteran Confederate troops. There were other engagements near Tallahassee, Lake City, and other Florida locales before the regiment was mustered out of service in October 1865.

The book also includes images of the Medal of Honor recipients of the next unit to leave Camp William Penn, the 6th Regiment USCT. On October 14, 1863, that regiment departed Camp William Penn under the leadership of Col. John W. Ames. This time, the brigade was allowed to parade through Philadelphia, with black and white crowds cheering them on, despite some elements of animosity in the crowd. Perhaps the fiercest regiment to originate from the camp, the 6th Regiment saw hellacious fighting at the Battle of New Market Heights or Chaffin's Farm in Virginia in September 1864. They also witnessed major action at Richmond, Petersburg, and Dutch Gap. Several of its members received the Medal of Honor at New Market Heights for saving the regiment's colors, including black sergeants Alexander Kelly and Thomas Hawkins, as well as Nathan H. Edgerton, a white lieutenant. Their images, among others, appear in this book. One of the most moving images in the book shows the proud black chaplain of the 6th, Rev. Jeremiah Asher, who wrote an autobiography telling of his grandfather's capture in Africa to be enslaved in America and later to serve in the Revolutionary War. Asher, who would become a founding member of Philadelphia's Shiloh Baptist Church, would decide to leave his wife and children to serve the soldiers of the 6th, but would not return home due to his death by disease in Wilmington, North Carolina, as the war wound down.

The horrific sacrifices in Olustee, Florida, of members of the 8th Regiment USCT, the next brigade to be trained at Camp William Penn, are a primary focus in this book. Images of commanding officers, such as Col. Charles W. Fribley, fatally wounded during the conflict, accompany accounts of the February 20, 1864, battle that resulted in many casualties. Yet, the book also has images of such black troops serving at Deep Bottom, Virginia, as well as New Market Heights or Chaffin's Farm, in late September 1864. The 8th would be among the first black troops to see Richmond begin to fall, as captured in various images, in March 1865, as well as participate in the pursuit of Confederate general Robert E. Lee. By April, the 8th would witness the surrender of Lee's army before being assigned to duty in the Rio Grande, Texas. They would be discharged on December 12, 1865, suffering by the end of the war tremendous losses totaling 251 men due to combat or disease.

Images of the mighty 22nd Regiment on the attack in Virginia, as well as being one of the first regiments to enter the conquered Confederate capital of Richmond, have been included. And the regiment's leading role in the funeral of Pres. Abraham Lincoln has also been a focus.

A plethora of valuable images have been preserved of the 25th Regiment USCT, organized at Camp William Penn in February 1864. Group pictures of the black recruits, as well as white officers, appear several places in this book, including the cover. The U.S. Army Military History Institute in Carlisle, Pennsylvania, allowed me access to dozens of individual photographic portraits of various officers and to some of the African American soldiers who served in several of the Civil War's major battles.

Other rare images of such Camp William Penn regiments as the 32nd, 41st, 43rd, 45th, and 127th show individual portraits as well as intense battle scenes. These regiments were engaged in Virginia, including the Battle of the Crater, operations at Petersburg and Richmond, the battles of Darbytown Road, Deep Bottom, and Fair Oaks, as well as Hatcher's Run. There was major service in South Carolina that encompassed Hilton Head, Port Royal, Otter Island, Fenwick Island, North Edisto Island, and James Island. Several of the regiments also pursued Lee's army and witnessed its surrender at Appomattox, as well as participated in Gen. William Tecumseh Sherman's epic campaign. Before being discharged, most would finally serve in Texas near the Mexican border, with at least a few ultimately joining the famed Buffalo soldiers.

By February 1865, the 24th Regiment was being organized at Camp William Penn where the men would hear a speech given by the great Underground Railroad matriarch, Harriet Tubman. According to the *Christian Recorder* newspaper, the soldiers "had a very entertaining homespun lecture from a colored woman known as Harriet Tubman. It was the first time [they] had the pleasure of hearing her," I reported in a November 1999 *America's Civil War* magazine article. "She seems to be very well known by the community at large, as the great Underground Rail Road woman, and has done a good part to many of her fellow creatures, in that direction."

It is a scene that epitomizes the essence of Camp William Penn and its warriors' participation in a war that broke the shackles of slavery and saved a nation.

One

Camp for Liberty

Virtually the entire Camp William Penn lays in the background as a solitary figure surveys the land known as Oak Farm, purchased by Lucretia Mott's son-in-law Edward M. Davis more than a decade before the Civil War. This photograph shows the facility surrounded by a high fence with a small party of people standing near what appears to be the main entrance to the camp. There is also a horse-drawn buggy and several tents to the left of buildings that appear to be the barracks. Initially, before the buildings were erected, the camp consisted primarily of tents, according to historical documents. The facility had been originally planned for a hilly area not far from Oak Farm, but was switched to the more level land of Davis's property that he leased to the federal government. (Historical Society of Pennsylvania.)

This rare photograph of Camp William Penn's main entrance with soldiers standing guard in the foreground and spectators posing near that entry was likely shot during the winter of 1863, 1864, or possibly 1865. Wagon tracks, human footprints, and horses' hoof imprints in the frozen

ground, as well as the overcoats of the onlookers, some possibly dignitaries, indicate the cold season. The lack of foliage on the trees is also a sign of the wintry season. (Historical Society of Pennsylvania.)

With the American flag fluttering to the right above trees devoid of leaves, more than a dozen onlookers seem to pose on the porch of what may be the barracks of Camp William Penn (Historical Society of Pennsylvania.)

Once known as the most recognized woman in the country, Lucretia Mott (1793–1880) was a legendary women's rights advocate and antislavery activist who lived adjacent to Camp William Penn in Chelten Hills. The facility stood on property that was owned by her son-in-law Edward M. Davis, a prominent member of the Union League of Philadelphia, which initially raised funds to establish Camp William Penn. Her Roadside estate became central to the Underground Railroad and attracted such prominent antislavery abolitionists as Frederick Douglass, William Lloyd Garrison, Sojourner Truth, and the great Harriet Tubman, to name a few. The Cheltenham Township neighborhood, formerly known as Chelten Hills, is today called LaMott in honor of Lucretia Mott, a Quaker with a deep and egalitarian religious intellect. (Library of Congress.)

This portrait of Jay Cooke (1821–1905), who financed the expenses of the Civil War for the Union by selling bonds, shows him as an older, but pensive, gentleman. The portrait hangs on the wall of the church he built and attended, St. Paul's Episcopal Church in Cheltenham Township, the same community where Camp William Penn was located. In fact, religious leaders and parishioners of the church reportedly helped the camp with spiritual matters, food, and other supplies. Cooke and many of his family members are buried in the church cemetery with an assortment of Civil War soldiers and officers. Adorned with Tiffany windows and the desk that Cooke worked on during the Civil War, St. Paul's was also attended by very wealthy families, including the Elkins and Wideners, who intermarried. A couple, in fact, died on the *Titanic* in 1912, including book collector Harry Widener, for whom Harvard University's library is named. (St. Paul's Episcopal Church.)

This striking depiction of Pres. Abraham Lincoln and a slave shows the leader holding his great Emancipation Proclamation as he encourages the black man to rise from bondage. It is a theme that resonated with the soldiers of Camp William Penn with at least one obliged to write to Lincoln during the war to complain about unequal medical treatment at the facility. Despite Lincoln's initial ambivalence about the use of black troops, he eventually succumbed to the demands of such top Union generals as George C. Freemont, who commanded the son-in-law of Lucretia Mott, Edward M. Davis. Davis and Mott were huge proponents of black liberty, demonstrated by the broken wrist shackles at the feet of Lincoln. (Library of Congress.)

The Union League of Philadelphia, as depicted in a watercolor by artist Frank H. Taylor, was located at 1118 Chestnut Street during most of the Civil War, from February 1863 to May 1865. Formerly known as the Hartman Kuhn residence, the organization was initially founded as a private club to support Pres. Abraham Lincoln's policies. Contributing more than $100,000 to the Union cause, the Union League also financially supported the establishment of Camp William Penn. Its prominent members included Edward M. Davis, Lucretia Mott's son-in-law, who leased the land where Camp William Penn would be erected to the federal government. Other noteworthy members hailed from many wealthy families of the time, including founders George Henry Boker, a highly esteemed poet and playwright, as well as jurist John Ines Clark Hare. (Bryn Mawr College Collections, gift of Joseph M. Fox.)

This photograph, taken of Louis Wagner (1883–1914) at age 23, a couple of years before he became commander of Camp William Penn in the summer of 1863, shows him with a relaxed demeanor. As a major in the 88th Pennsylvania Infantry Regiment, his right shin was shattered by a Confederate bullet during the Second Battle of Bull Run on August 30, 1862. The 24-year-old was captured but later released via a prisoner exchange. The German-born Wagner before then had fought in the battles of Groveton, Thoroughfare Gap, Rappahannock Station, and Cedar Mountain. Meanwhile, he quickly rose in rank, from captain and lieutenant colonel to colonel and finally brigadier general by the end of the war. Wagner steadfastly supported his black troops, even when one black sentry at the camp was convicted of shooting and killing an intruding neighborhood man in August 1863. Wagner also protested the segregated treatment of his black soldiers, as well as the brutality that some suffered while in Philadelphia. (U.S. Army Military History Institute.)

This watercolor by artist Frank H. Taylor captures pedestrians in 1863 walking by the "Officers' School for Colored Troops," also known as the Free Military School for the Applicants for the Command of Colored Troops, 1210 Chestnut Street, Philadelphia. Two white officers appear to be exchanging words with a black recruit on the pavement as a soldier stands guard at the door. (Bryn Mawr College Collections, gift of Joseph M. Fox.)

This emotional 1863 poster image of a black Civil War soldier targeted slaves, many inspired to join regiments at Camp William Penn starting midsummer of 1863. It appealed to their desire for emancipation, to attend public school, and receive an education, as well as the right to own property. Yet the most potent message was to join the fight to save the Union that would ultimately lead to overall liberty for blacks. (Library Company of Philadelphia.)

Octavius V. Catto (1839–1871) was one of the most influential and articulate black activists in Philadelphia and known in African American communities throughout the country. He helped to recruit black soldiers for Camp William Penn's 3rd Regiment, the first unit to be established at the facility during midsummer of 1863. Catto had relocated to Philadelphia from Charleston, South Carolina, with his family as a young child under the guidance of his father, William Catto, a black preacher with many ties to the antislavery abolitionist community. As a young man, Catto became a renowned scholar, educator, and administrator at the Institute for Colored Youth, the predecessor of Cheyney University, and a member of the scientific powerhouse, the Franklin Institute, a pioneering and noteworthy accomplishment for an African American. He also established a black baseball team, the Pythians, the first to formally play a white team in Philadelphia, and became a leader in desegregating the city's public facilities, including streetcars. He was assassinated in October 1871 for encouraging blacks to vote, resulting in one of the largest funerals in Philadelphia history that attracted thousands of whites and African Americans. (Library of Congress.)

The African Methodist Episcopalian Church (AME) played an important political, social, and spiritual role in the lives of the black soldiers of Camp William Penn during the Civil War. Chief among them was educator and church activist Bishop Daniel A. Payne. (General Research and Reference Division, Schomburg Center for Research in Black Culture, the New York Public Library; Astor, Lenox, and Tilden Foundations.)

MEN OF COLOR

TO ARMS! TO ARMS!

NOW OR NEVER

This is our golden moment! The Government of the United States calls for every Able-bodied Colored Man to enter the Army for the

Three Years' Service!

And join in Fighting the Battles of Liberty and the Union. A new era is open to us. For generations we have suffered under the horrors of slavery, outrage and wrong; our manhood has been denied, our citizenship blotted out, our souls seared and burned, our spirits cowed and crushed, and the hopes of the future of our race involved in doubt and darkness. But now our relations to the white race are changed. Now, therefore, is our most precious moment. Let us rush to arms!

FAIL NOW, & OUR RACE IS DOOMED

On this the soil of our birth. We must now awake, arise, or be forever fallen. If we value liberty, if we wish to be free in this land, if we love our country, if we love our families, our children, our home, we must strike *now* while the country calls: we must rise up in the dignity of our manhood, and show by our own right arms that we are worthy to be freemen. Our enemies have made the country believe that we are craven cowards, without soul, without manhood, without the spirit of soldiers. Shall we die with this stigma resting upon our graves? Shall we leave this inheritance of Shame to our Children? No! a thousand times NO! We WILL Rise! The alternative is upon us. Let us rather die freemen than live to be slaves. What is life without liberty? We say that we have manhood; now is the time to prove it. A nation or a people that cannot fight may be pitied, but cannot be respected. If we would be regarded *men*, if we would forever silence the tongue of Calumny, of Prejudice and Hate, let us Rise Now and Fly to Arms! We have seen what Valor and Heroism our Brothers displayed at Port Hudson and Milliken's Bend, though they are just from the galling, poisoning grasp of Slavery, they have startled the World by the most exalted heroism. If they have proved themselves heroes, cannot WE PROVE OURSELVES MEN!

ARE FREEMEN LESS BRAVE THAN SLAVES

More than a Million White Men have left Comfortable Homes and joined the Armies of the Union to save their Country. Cannot we leave ours, and swell the Hosts of the Union, to save our liberties, vindicate our manhood, and deserve well of our Country. MEN OF COLOR! the Englishman, the Irishman, the Frenchman, the German, the American, have been called to assert their claim to freedom and a manly character, by an appeal to the sword. The day that has seen an enslaved race in arms has, in all history, seen their last trial. We now see that our last opportunity has come. If we are not lower in the scale of humanity than Englishmen, Irishmen, White Americans and other Races, we can show it now. Men of Color, Brothers and Fathers, we appeal to you, by all your concern for yourselves and your liberties, by all your regard for God and humanity, by all your desire for Citizenship and Equality before the law, by all your love for the Country, to stop at no subterfuge, listen to nothing that shall deter you from rallying for the Army. Come Forward, and at once Enroll your Names for the Three Years' Service. Strike now, and you are henceforth and forever Freemen!

E. D. Bassett,	Rev. J. Underdue,	P. J. Armstrong,	Rev. J. C. Gibbs,	Elijah J. Davis,
William D. Forten,	John W. Price,	J. W. Simpson,	Daniel George,	John P. Burr,
Frederick Douglass,	Augustus Dorsey,	Rev. J. B. Trusty,	Robert M. Adger,	Robert Jones,
Wm. Whipper,	Rev. Stephen Smith,	S. Morgan Smith,	Henry M. Cropper,	O. V. Catto,
D. D. Turner,	N. W. Depee,	William E. Gipson,	Rev. J. B. Reeve,	Thos. J. Dorsey,
Jas. McCrummell,	Dr. J. H. Wilson,	Rev. J. Boulden,	Rev. J. A. Williams,	I. D. Cliff,
A. S. Cassey,	J. W. Cassey,	Rev. J. Asher,	Rev. A. L. Stanford,	Jacob C. White,
A. M. Green,	James Needham,	Rev. Elisha Weaver,	Thomas J. Bowers,	Morris Hall,
J. W. Page,	Ebenezer Black,	David B. Bowser,	J. C. White, Jr.,	J. P. Johnson,
L. R. Seymour,	James R. Gordon,	Henry Minton,	Rev. J. P. Campbell,	Franklin Turner,
Rev. William T. Catto,	Samuel Stewart,	Daniel Colley,	Rev. W. J. Alston,	Jesse E. Glasgow.

A Meeting in furtherance of the above named object will be held

And will be Addressed by

U. S. Steam-Power Book and Job Printing Establishment, Ledger Buildings, Third and Chestnut Streets, Philadelphia.

One of the most effective recruiting weapons for black troops during the Civil War, this "Men of Color" broadside appealed to and convinced many of the first black men to fill the regimental rolls at Camp William Penn. Its words evoked the horrors of slavery, advocated saving the future for black children, and disproved claims that African American men were cowardly and unintelligent. If white men could leave "comfortable" homes to defend the Union, then black men could also "prove" themselves as "men." Very notable are the names of some of the most powerful and respected antislavery abolitionist leaders in the region, including Frederick Douglass, William Whipper, Rev. Stephen Smith, Rev. Jeremiah Asher, and Rev. W. J. Alston, as well as Rev. William T. Catto and his son, Octavius V. Catto, who was killed by a white assassin's bullet while advocating for black suffrage in October 1871. (Gilder Lehrman Institute of American History.)

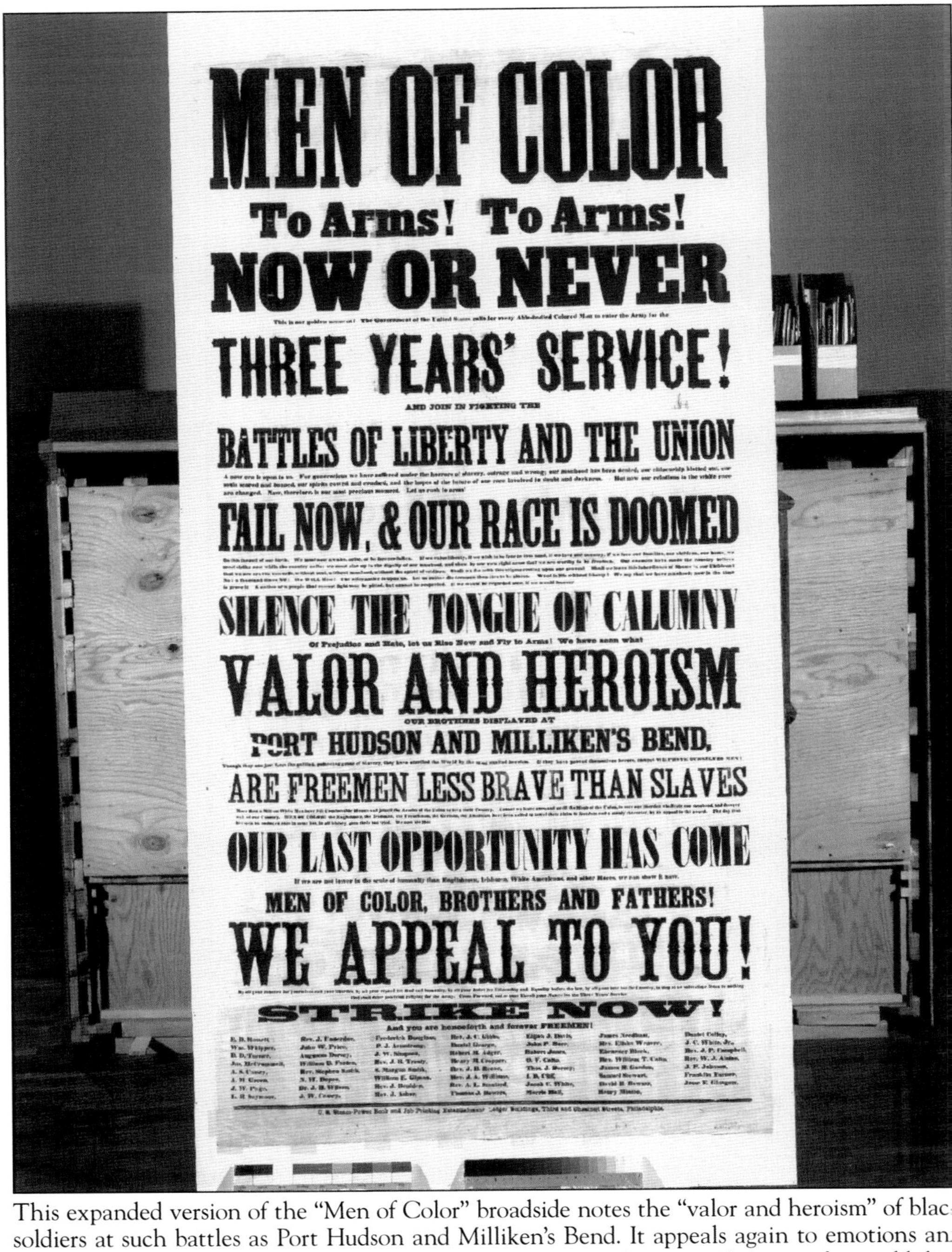

This expanded version of the "Men of Color" broadside notes the "valor and heroism" of black soldiers at such battles as Port Hudson and Milliken's Bend. It appeals again to emotions and emphasizes urgency with the words, "Our last opportunity has come." Again, for credibility, prominent blacks—primarily in the Philadelphia region—are listed to encourage black recruitment, especially at Camp William Penn. (Library Company of Philadelphia.)

This lithograph drawing appeared in the *National Guard* newspaper of Philadelphia on Saturday, July 18, 1863, depicting the great activity at Camp William Penn. As the image shows, the facility became quite a spectacle for the surrounding communities, including nearby Philadelphia. Many of the men's wives and partners would visit the camp, attracting especially large crowds when parades or drills were scheduled. Observers would travel by horse and buggy, as well as via segregated trains and horse-drawn trolleys. (Union League of Philadelphia.)

This lithograph of Camp William Penn depicts soldiers on parade or drilling, likely in late 1863 or 1864. A commander, possibly the camp's top officer, Lt. Col. Louis Wagner, rides on horseback in the foreground with several nearby soldiers on patrol as two American flags flutter over the camp's building and the horizon of Chelten Hills. The scene was likely captured during the early fall or late spring since the trees still have foliage and smoke from the chimneys is rising into the skies. (Free Library of Philadelphia.)

This very rare photograph of Camp William Penn soldiers was the model for an extremely popular recruiting poster. The picture of 25th Regiment United States Colored Troops recruits and an officer, resembling the camp commander Louis Wagner, was likely shot during early 1864 in Philadelphia. The photograph, discovered by Maryland-based scholar Dr. James Spina, was so striking that an artist superimposed images of the wooded background, a tent, and an American flag, similar to Camp William Penn's setting in Chelten Hills (see page 2). There is also an artist's rendition of a young drummer superimposed in the lithograph engraved by P. S. Duval and Son in Philadelphia. Many years later, the original photograph was retouched by Confederate sympathizers depicting the soldiers as the 1st Louisiana Native Guard, initially an all-black Confederate unit, according to Jerome Handler, senior scholar of the Virginia Foundation for the Humanities and Michael L. Tuite Jr., former director of the Digital Media Lab at the University of Virginia. (Dr. James Spina.)

This photograph of Camp William Penn may have been the model of an artist's lithograph depiction of the camp as an American flag flutters above an array of buildings with a lone soldier standing in the foreground in front of a high fence encircling the camp. With the trees appearing to lose some foliage and the sky somewhat overcast, the photograph was likely taken in the fall or winter of 1863 or 1864, possibly 1865. (National Archives.)

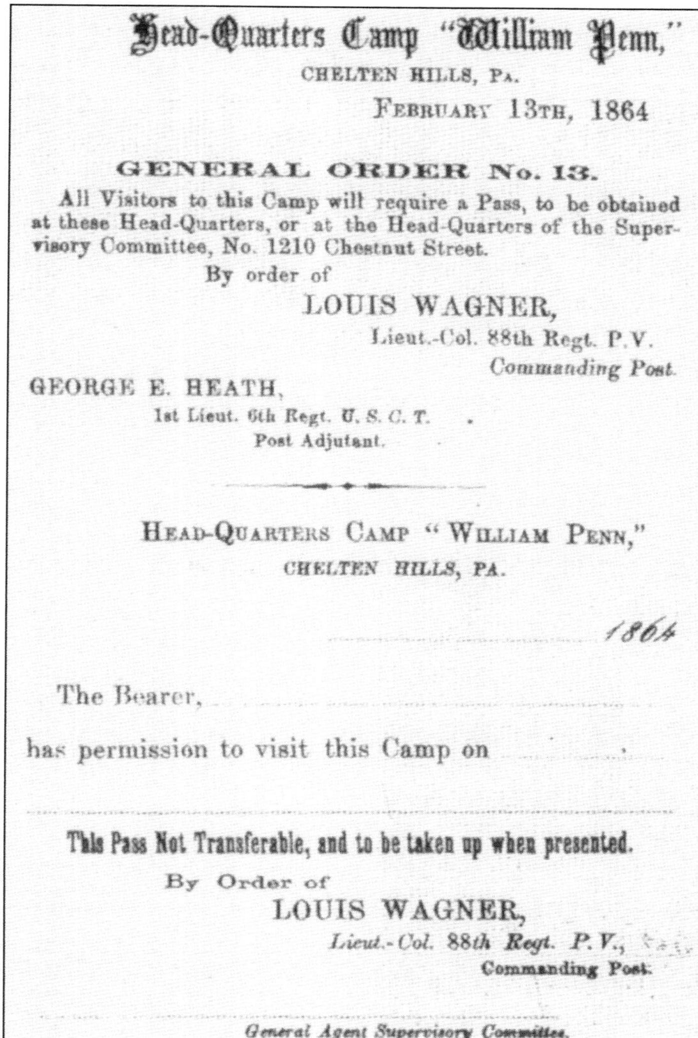

Head-Quarters Camp "William Penn,"

CHELTEN HILLS, PA.

FEBRUARY 13TH, 1864

GENERAL ORDER No. 13.

All Visitors to this Camp will require a Pass, to be obtained at these Head-Quarters, or at the Head-Quarters of the Supervisory Committee, No. 1210 Chestnut Street.

By order of

LOUIS WAGNER,

Lieut.-Col. 88th Regt. P.V.

Commanding Post.

GEORGE E. HEATH,

1st Lieut. 6th Regt. U. S. C. T.

Post Adjutant.

HEAD-QUARTERS CAMP "WILLIAM PENN,"

CHELTEN HILLS, PA.

1864

The Bearer,

has permission to visit this Camp on

This Pass Not Transferable, and to be taken up when presented.

By Order of

LOUIS WAGNER,

Lieut.-Col. 88th Regt. P. V.,

Commanding Post.

General Agent Supervisory Committee.

The visitor's pass for Camp William Penn bears the name of the facility's commander Lt. Col. Louis Wagner, who suffered a severe leg injury at the Second Battle of Bull Run and volunteered to command the camp in the summer of 1863. Also listed is George E. Heath, the post adjutant, then a first lieutenant of the 6th Regiment United States Colored Troops (USCT), one of the fiercest fighting units from Camp William Penn with several members earning the Medal of Honor at the Battle of New Market Heights or Chaffin's Farm. (U.S. Army Military History Institute.)

ON PICKET DUTY.

115

This black soldier on picket duty is reminiscent of a tragic event that happened at Camp William Penn on August 10, 1863, when a private was forced to shoot an intruding white resident of the surrounding community, William Fox. After Fox refused to listen to Pvt. Charles A. Ridley's orders to leave the fence area being guarded to thwart intrusions and desertions, Ridley fired. The camp's commander, Louis Wagner, at first refused to turn over Ridley to authorities. However, charges were eventually brought and Ridley was arrested, media reports indicate. He served a short time in prison before being released. Ridley was reportedly mustered out with his unit at the end of the war. (General Research and Reference Division, Schomburg Center for Research in Black Culture, the New York Public Library; Astor, Lenox, and Tilden Foundations.)

This lithograph was likely patterned after an original photograph of Camp William Penn. The caption reads, "Rendezvous for United States Colored Troops. City Line [now Cheltenham Avenue], Near North Pennsylvania Railroad, Chelten Hills, Pa." Col. Louis Wagner of the 88th is given credit for commanding the facility. (U.S. Army Military History Institute.)

Military Hall in downtown Philadelphia near the customhouse was a noted bar and refreshment stop for Civil War soldiers. Artist Frank H. Taylor, via watercolors, shows much activity in the area, including food and newspaper vendors. The building was probably a familiar sight to the men on their way to transportation depots or the waterfront to catch a steam vessel to war. (Bryn Mawr College Collections, gift of Joseph M. Fox.)

Above, the Union Volunteer Refreshment Saloon sometimes hosted black Camp William Penn troops who paraded to such places—at first with great opposition from whites fearing retribution for slavery and bigotry. Below, an image of Jay Cooke and Company, a finance firm owned by Jay Cooke, the "financier of the Civil War" for the Union, shows much hustle and bustle. Cooke's mansion, Ogontz, was located not far from Camp William Penn in Chelten Hills. Pres. Ulysses S. Grant visited Cooke's mansion while the former general's son, Jesse, was enrolled at a local military academy near Camp William Penn. (Free Library of Philadelphia.)

This depiction of the Union Volunteer Refreshment Saloon shows the immense activity there and in the general area of that Washington Avenue locale. Today not far from here is the Italian market of outside food vendors and specialty food stores. Some Camp William Penn soldiers wrote letters indicating that they had eaten and been served refreshments in the dining saloon. (Free Library of Philadelphia.)

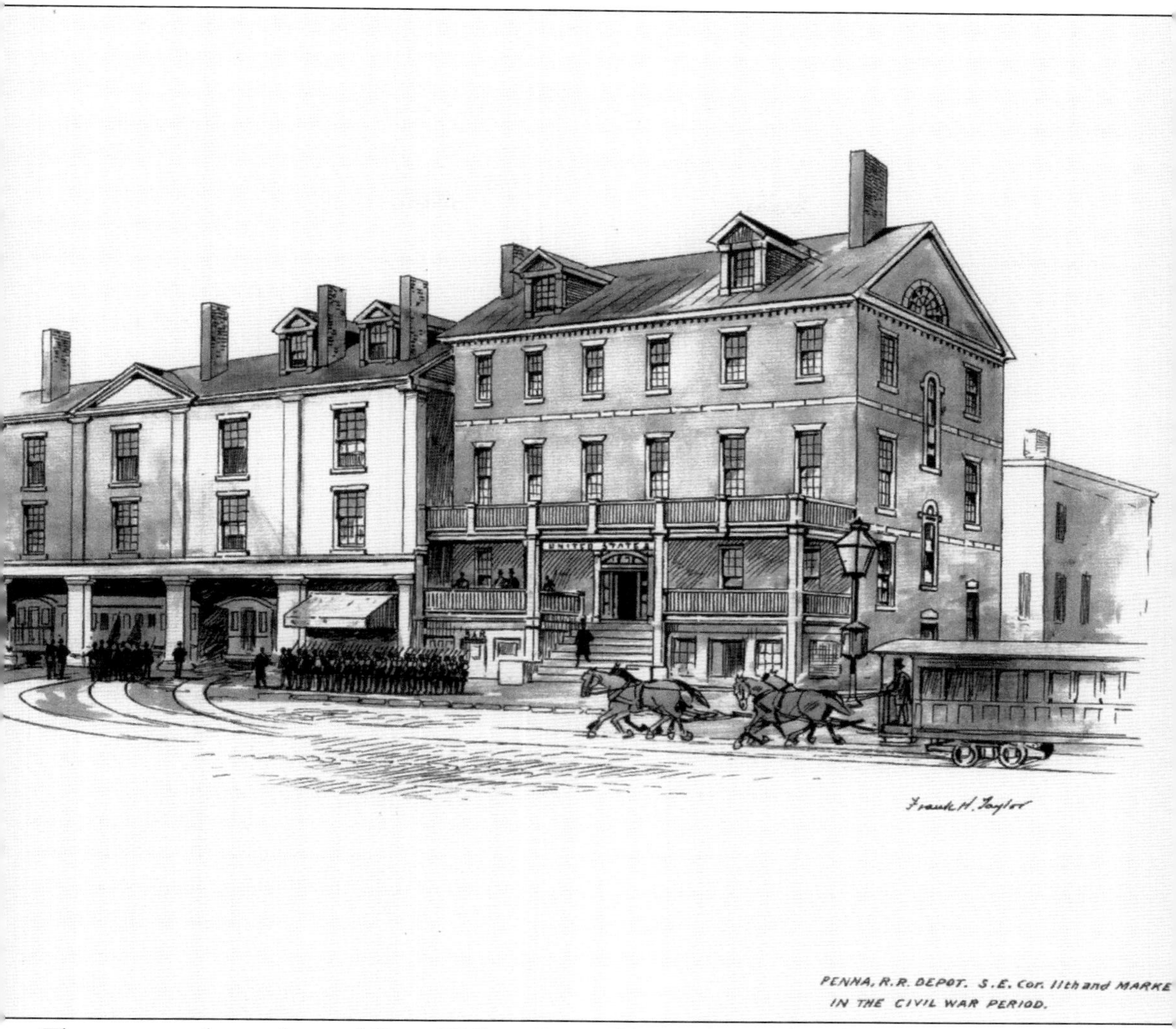

The correspondence of several Camp William Penn soldiers indicates that they were transported by railroad from the Pennsylvania Railroad depot at Eleventh and Market Streets in downtown Philadelphia, although as passengers being segregated. This Frank H. Taylor watercolor depicts one of the numerous horse-drawn vehicles that were used to transport citizens to see Camp William Penn soldiers parade on weekends, often with blacks having to ride on platforms outside of the passenger cabin. Lucretia Mott and Camp William Penn's commander Louis Wagner protested such segregation. (Bryn Mawr College Collections, gift of Joseph M. Fox.)

Abolitionist John Brown sometimes communicated with the Quaker antislavery abolitionist Lucretia Mott, who lived adjacent to the camp, before leading the insurrection at Harper's Ferry on October 16, 1859. His wife Mary was harbored at the Mott family estate, Roadside, as Brown was hung on December 2, 1859, after being cornered by West Point graduate Robert E. Lee, the future general of the Confederate army. (Library of Congress.)

The antislavery abolitionists who visited Camp William Penn, including Lucretia Mott, Harriet Tubman, and Frederick Douglass, would have preferred remembering John Brown as sagacious and ruggedly handsome, as depicted in this replication of Martin M. Lawrence's original photograph. Douglass and Tubman personally feared charges of conspiracy following Brown's since they had communicated with Brown beforehand, but decided to distance themselves. (Library of Congress.)

John Brown was characterized as a demon and savior in proslavery and antislavery publications throughout the country, even after his death. This depiction shows disdain for Brown's hangman, who is deceptively attired in women's clothing. It is a depiction that would have likely riled Lucretia Mott, a fierce women's rights advocate even when she lived next to Camp William Penn. (Library of Congress.)

Martial law was declared in Kansas when the antislavery abolitionist John Brown confronted proslavery forces as early as the mid-1850s when the likes of Lancaster's Gerrit Smith, a local supporter of Camp William Penn and the antislavery abolitionist movement, collected donations for weapons and ammunition for Brown. (Library of Congress.)

John Brown's second wife, Mary A. Brown, took refuge at Lucretia Mott's Roadside estate when her husband was tried and ultimately executed on December 2, 1859. Mary wrote a letter to her children while at Mott's home, indicating that their father was standing brave in the face of his likely doom. "I am here with Mrs. Lucretia Mott where I expect to stay until your dear father is dispose of," she wrote in the November 28, 1859, letter. "O what a terrible thought. . . . But may the god of all peace be with us all as he is with him." (Library of Congress.)

William Still, "father of the Underground Railroad," delivered coal to the camp and served as post sutler. Still had carefully documented the escapes of hundreds of runaway slaves who were shuttled through his Philadelphia home, many of them relayed to Lucretia Mott's Roadside next to Camp William Penn. Still eventually wrote a landmark book based on his notes, titled *The Underground Railroad.* (Library of Congress.)

PETER STILL,

THE KIDNAPPED AND RANSOMED.

While operating the major Philadelphia station of the Underground Railroad, William Still miraculously met his brother Peter, who had been separated from him and other family members when they were slaves. Peter had come to William's home to seek refuge when the two realized that they were brothers. (Library Company of Philadelphia.)

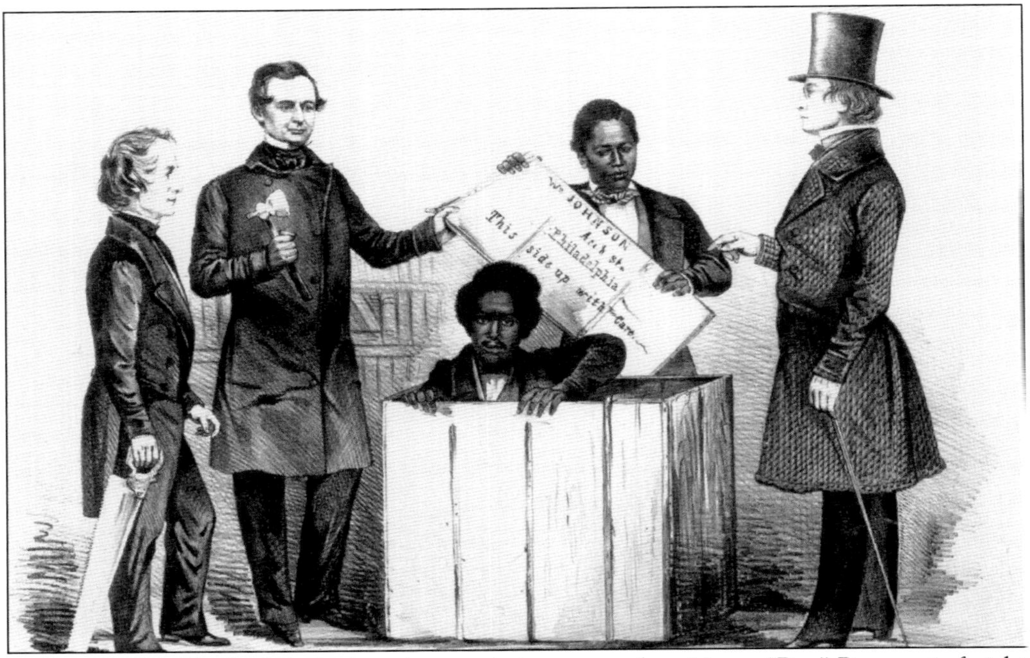

William Still holds the lid of a box that carried runaway slave Henry "Box" Brown via freight train to Philadelphia in a box shipped from Virginia in March 1849. Their Underground Railroad activities persisted throughout the Civil War and likely included helping black troops of Camp William Penn to reach freedom. One slave catcher was repulsed from the camp by soldiers. (Library Company of Philadelphia.)

Thomas Morris Chester was the first black newspaper correspondent for a large daily newspaper, the *Philadelphia Press*. The Harrisburg native wrote dispatches about many of the battles in which Camp William Penn regiments participated. Also noted as a lawyer and politician, Chester helped to recruit black troops and traveled extensively abroad to raise money via pro-Union speeches. (Library of Congress.)

Gen. John C. Fremont (1813–1890) commanded Capt. Edward M. Davis, the son-in-law of Lucretia Mott, in the U.S. Army just before the Civil War. Stationed with Davis in Missouri, Freemont issued a proclamation in 1861 to free the area's slaves, possibly a prelude to Lincoln's future Emancipation Proclamation. Calling the initiative premature, Lincoln halted it. The former explorer of Western territories was later nominated for president by the Republican Party in 1856 with support of abolitionists. (Library of Congress.)

William Lloyd Garrison (1805–1879), the most well-known European American antislavery abolitionist of his time, visited Lucretia Mott's home and corresponded with her by letter. A prolific newspaper editor and writer who initially collaborated with Frederick Douglass, Garrison edited the *Liberator* newspaper and believed that the U.S. Constitution was a proslavery document. Garrison maintained very friendly ties with Lucretia Mott, forming such powerful groups as the Anti-Slavery Society. (Library of Congress.)

Shown in formal attire, William Lloyd Garrison vigorously supported the recruitment of black troops during the Civil War, including at Camp William Penn. In his paper, the *Liberator*, he ran a routine column, "Chronicle of the War," and published bulletins about Frederick Douglass's ongoing efforts to recruit black troops in Pennsylvania, Ohio, Massachusetts, and other states. (National Archives.)

Elizabeth Greenfield Taylor, born a slave between 1817 and 1831, was an educator and very popular singer who performed at concerts to raise funds for black troops of Camp William Penn, as well as for various abolitionist causes. Known as the "Black Swan," she was born in Natchez, Mississippi. She was freed after her owner, widow Elizabeth Holliday Greenfield, moved to Philadelphia and became a Quaker. (Library of Congress.)

Thomas J. Bowers's name appears in the "Men of Color" broadside to recruit black soldiers for Camp William Penn in Philadelphia with more than 50 other prominent black leaders of the day. Bowers performed at benefits to help raise money to recruit black troops along with Elizabeth Greenfield Taylor, the "Black Swan." Known as the "Colored Mario," Bowers was noted for his wonderful tenor voice. (Library of Congress.)

William Whipper was a wealthy and staunch antislavery abolitionist who lived in Pennsylvania's Lancaster County in the town of Columbia and fervently supported the establishment of Camp William Penn. Also active in the Underground Railroad, Whipper received hundreds of runaway slaves at his home. His name is listed on the "Men of Color" broadside to recruit black soldiers for Camp William Penn. (Library of Congress.)

Robert Purvis, born free in 1810, was a very wealthy black abolitionist of mixed ancestry who was extremely close to local Philadelphia abolitionists. He staunchly supported the troops at Camp William Penn, often visiting and speaking there as well as paying visits to Lucretia Mott at her nearby home. He died in 1898 and is buried near Mott at the Fairhill Cemetery in Philadelphia. (Library of Congress.)

Caroline Still was the daughter of William Still, forever linked to the Underground Railroad system of harboring escaped slaves. Due to her father's business savvy, including operating a supply store at Camp William Penn, she attended several private schools as a child and the Institute for Coloured Youth in Philadelphia, the forerunner of Cheyney University. She later became a physician, graduating from Women's Medical College of Pennsylvania in March 1878. (Library of Congress.)

James and Lucretia Mott married in 1811 after the two met as teachers at Nine Partners Quaker School in Dutchess County, New York, and James became a business partner of Lucretia's father, Thomas. They became lifelong egalitarian partners with James supporting Lucretia's antislavery abolitionist and women's rights activities. The couple had six surviving children and started Swarthmore College and Women's Medical College of Pennsylvania. (Friends Historical Library at Swarthmore College.)

Lucretia is seen here sitting with family members. Standing to the top left is daughter Maria Mott Davis, married to Edward M. Davis, who helped raise funds for Camp William Penn and on whose land the facility was built. Granddaughter Anna Davis Hallowell, the daughter of Maria Mott Davis, stands in back of Lucretia, to the right. Finally, there is Mott's great-granddaughter Maria Hallowell, the daughter of Anna. (Friends Historical Library at Swarthmore College.)

Lucretia Mott, seated in a chair, is shown with family members at her Roadside estate, likely after the Civil War. Camp William Penn would have been situated at the rear of the home in the midst of rolling hills and farmland. This made the home an ideal location for harboring runaway slaves via the Underground Railroad. Sitting beside Mott is likely her daughter, Maria Mott Davis, who was married to Edward M. Davis, a member of the Union League of Philadelphia. Granddaughter Anna Davis Hallowell, the daughter of Maria Mott Davis, is likely standing to the left near the tree. A grandchild sits on the ground on what appears to be a blanket. (Friends Historical Library at Swarthmore College.)

The Quaker poet, writer, and journalist John Greenleaf Whittier (1807–1892) attended many antislavery meetings with Lucretia Mott. An ardent abolitionist, Whittier was editor of the abolitionist paper *Pennsylvania Freeman*, with its primary office in Philadelphia at the antislavery meeting place Pennsylvania Hall before it was set afire in 1838 by proslavery advocates. Over the ensuing years, Whittier supported Mott's antislavery initiatives locally and on the national level. They had mutual lifelong friends, including the great William Lloyd Garrison, who published Whittier's poem *The Exile's Departure* at the age of 19. (Friends Historical Library at Swarthmore College.)

Edward M. Davis, son-in-law of the Quaker antislavery abolitionist Lucretia Mott, was married to her daughter Maria Mott Davis. Just before the Civil War, he had served on the staff of Gen. John C. Freemont. Both shared antislavery views. Davis helped Frederick Douglass escape slavery and owned the land where Camp William Penn was erected. His son William Morris Davis would become "the father of American geography." (Friends Historical Library at Swarthmore College.)

At her Roadside home, Lucretia Mott often entertained the country's most well-known abolitionists. William Lloyd Garrison visited Roadside several times and supported the raising of black troops at Camp William Penn. George Thompson, an abolitionist based in England, was close to Garrison and Mott and spoke out against slavery early on in England and the United States. Wendell Phillips also visited Mott's home and supported antislavery abolitionist causes. (Friends Historical Library at Swarthmore College.)

Known as an antislavery writer, poet, lecturer, and political activist, Frances Ellen Watkins Harper (1825–1911) was an associate of Lucretia Mott. She gave support to Mary Brown, the wife of abolitionist John Brown, when he was imprisoned following the unsuccessful Harper's Ferry uprising in 1859. It was not uncommon to see such women of color visit Mott's Roadside estate, adjacent to Camp William Penn. (Library of Congress.)

Mifflin Wistar Gibbs was an important agent of the Underground Railroad who had ties to Lucretia Mott and other conductors during the Civil War era. Historian Charles Blockson notes that Gibbs ultimately pioneered in California and British Columbia, eventually settling in Little Rock, Arkansas, in 1871. Gibbs was the first black to be elected as a municipal judge there and ultimately became a U.S. consul in Madagascar, Blockson notes. (Library of Congress.)

William Howard Day when young
Reprinted from B. F. Wheeler, *Cullings From Zion's Poets*

William Howard Day was very active on the Underground Railroad and likely helped runaway slaves, via Lucretia Mott's Roadside stop, get to Canada. Although he was born in New York City, he traveled extensively throughout North America and Britain, speaking out against the horrors of slavery. He eventually became an educator in Harrisburg, rising to become president of the district's school board from 1891 to 1893. (Library of Congress.)

The first black to rise to the rank of major in the U.S. Army during the Civil war era, Martin R. Delany (1812–1885) helped to convince Pres. Abraham Lincoln to recruit African American troops, including at Camp William Penn. The multitalented Delany was also very active with the Underground Railroad, as well as working as a physician, author, and editor. The Pittsburgh native edited the black newspaper in his hometown, the *Mystery*; he also served as editor of the *North Star*, Frederick Douglass's newspaper. (Library of Congress.)

Harriet Tubman, the supreme conductor of the Underground Railroad, spoke to the 24th Regiment USCT in April 1865 at Camp William Penn and several times visited Lucretia Mott's nearby home during the Civil War era. Tubman, who was also an army scout, nurse, and intelligence gatherer, encouraged soldiers of the 24th in a down-home black dialect, noted newspaper reporters. Tubman, who had escaped the cruelty of slavery in Maryland years earlier and found work in Philadelphia, often ushered slaves to such stations as Mott's nearby Roadside estate before they were moved on to Lancaster or even Canada. (Library of Congress.)

Jacob C. White was a major operator of the Underground Railroad who kept records at a cemetery that he owned. The adept businessman was a close friend to black activist Octavius V. Catto, assassinated on October 10, 1871, while fighting for African American rights. They both supported black troops at Camp William Penn and were members of the Vigilant Committee, many of them signers of Civil War broadsides to recruit black soldiers for the war. (Library of Congress.)

Bishop Benjamin T. Tanner of the AME Church, seated in the middle of the picture with his family, vehemently supported the black troops during the Civil War, including at Camp William Penn. His son Henry Tanner, standing to the left, became one of America's best-known artists. Seated to Tanner's right is his wife, Sarah Elizabeth. The AME church had historic ties to Philadelphia where it was started during the late 1700s by Bishop Richard Allen, an ex-slave. (Library of Congress.)

Henry Ossawa Tanner (1859–1937), the celebrated black artist, was inspired to paint while walking through a Philadelphia park with his father, Bishop Benjamin T. Tanner of the AME Church, who was also the editor of the *Christian Recorder*. It was a newspaper of the AME Church that often printed letters of Camp William Penn soldiers from the battlefront during the Civil War. (Library of Congress.)

The prolific orator and black freedom fighter Sojourner Truth (about 1799–1883) collaborated with Lucretia Mott in organizing groups to combat opponents of slavery's abolishment and increased women's rights. Author of the *Narrative of Sojourner Truth* about her rise from slavery to become a powerful liberation advocate, she became an itinerant preacher who often met with Mott. During the Civil War, in 1864, Truth also met with Pres. Abraham Lincoln. (Library of Congress.)

Two

FREEDOM'S WARRIORS

David Bustill Bowser (1820–1900) designed and created the regimental flags of Camp William Penn. Although he painted well-known portraits of Abraham Lincoln and abolitionist John Brown, the self-taught artist worked early on as a sign painter, according to historian Charles Blockson, and produced "landscapes, portraits, emblems, and banners for local organizations such as firemen's groups," says Blockson's 2001 book *African-Americans in Pennsylvania*. Most of the flags have not survived, with some reportedly being intentionally destroyed following the war. (Library of Congress.)

The motto on the obverse flag that Bowser designed and created for the 3rd Regiment USCT, the first to leave Camp William Penn during the summer of 1863, lives today via reenactors dedicated to "Rather die freemen, than live to be slaves." The foreground depicts a soldier protecting the honor of Lady Liberty. (Library of Congress.)

The 3rd Regiment's flag indicates that it was presented to the group "by a committee of ladies of Philadelphia" in October 1863. Painted by Bowser, the flag "was prepared by the special order of our patriotic colored ladies of Philadelphia," reported the *Christian Recorder* newspaper. The American eagle is displayed with the immortal words, *E Pluribus Unum*, which means "one for many," representing the country's unity. (Library of Congress.)

Profiling is an escaped slave who enlisted in the Union army, similar to many of the black recruits at Camp William Penn. More than a few of the soldiers bore the wounds of slavery, including whip lashes and even castration. Abolitionists Frederick Douglass and Harriet Tubman, speakers at the camp, both bore the scars of slavery. (Picture Collection, the Branch Libraries, the New York Public Library, Astor, Lenox, and Tilden Foundations.)

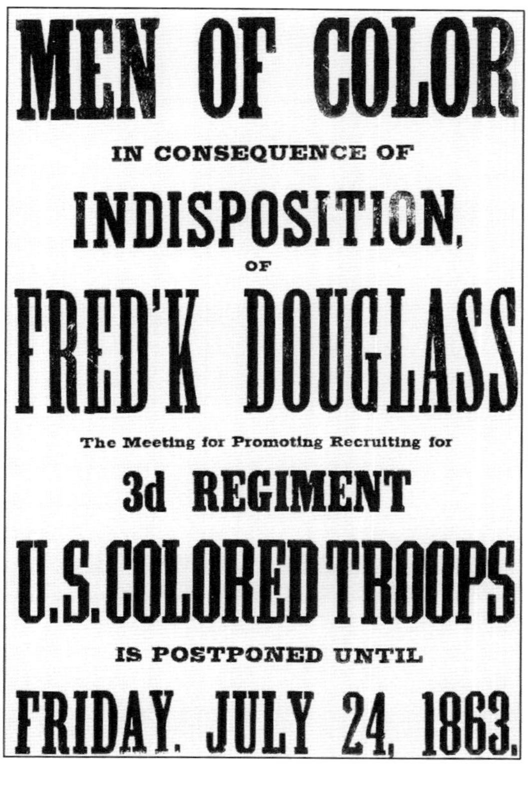

Although the great black abolitionist Frederick Douglass was scheduled to speak at Camp William Penn on July 18, 1863, the event was rescheduled for almost a week later, according to this poster. Douglass, a paid recruiter for the Union army, spoke to the men of the 3rd Regiment USCT about the importance of their combat mission that would directly impact the freedom of millions of African Americans. (U.S. Army Military History Institute.)

Lt. Col. Ulysses Doubleday mustered into service on October 2, 1863, joining the 3rd Regiment USCT. He was promoted from lieutenant colonel of the 3rd Regiment to colonel of the 45th Regiment USCT on October 5, 1864. His men fired the last shot at Lee's army. He was promoted to brevet brigadier general on March 11, 1865, and later discharged by special order. (U.S. Army Military History Institute.)

January 16, 1865, was the day 2nd Lt. Benjamin Frank Roberts mustered into service. He joined Company D of the 3rd Regiment USCT at Camp William Penn. He was mustered out of the company on October 31, 1865. (U.S. Army Military History Institute.)

On August 11, 1863, 1st Lt. Cyrus W. Brown originally mustered in and joined the 3rd Regiment USCT's Company K before being promoted to adjutant on June 23, 1865 He was mustered out on October 31, 1865. (U.S. Army Military History Institute.)

Capt. Alex S. Toplanyi was mustered into service on August 21, 1863, joining the 3rd Regiment USCT's Company F at the camp. The brigade served in South Carolina at Forts Gregg and Wagner on Morris Island in September 1863, several months after the black regiment, the Massachusetts 54th, valiantly succumbed to rebel forces at Wagner. Black troops of the 3rd were hung in Florida following a dispute with local whites just after the war. (U.S. Army Military History Institute.)

COLORED MEN ENGAGED IN BATTLE, PETERSBURG, VA.

Several of Camp William Penn's regiments battled in Petersburg, Virginia, including the 43rd, 45th, and 8th. This depiction shows troops fighting in close quarters with Confederate troops. The combat was especially fierce during the Battle of the Crater, on July 30, 1864. One observer described the velocity and thickness of bullets as so acute that they collided in midair. During that engagement, many black soldiers were killed, including from the 43rd, when Union forces planted explosives under the Confederate stronghold, resulting in a massive explosion. Although many Confederate soldiers were killed, the resulting chaos allowed those forces to rebound and inflict heavy casualties. (Manuscripts, Archives and Rare Books Division, Schomburg Center for Research in Black Culture, the New York Public Library; Astor, Lenox, and Tilden Foundations.)

The Reverend Jeremiah Asher joined the 6th Regiment USCT as a chaplain after migrating from New England where his grandfather had been a slave. In an autobiography, Asher tells the story of how his granddad was captured in Africa and placed on a slave ship destined for Connecticut. His grandfather agreed to fight in the Revolutionary War in place of his so-called master in exchange for freedom. However, following the war, his owner reneged and Asher's grandfather was forced to work for more years and pay the man an exorbitant fee for his freedom. Asher wrote of the great wisdom and religious tenacity he had learned from his grandfather, Gad, who had become blind. It is that religious zeal and advocacy for black equality that likely led Jeremiah Asher to become a founding pastor of the Shiloh Baptist Church in Philadelphia and to later temporarily leave his wife and children to serve the men of 6th, many of them ex-slaves. However, Asher would never return home. As the war ended, Asher died in 1865 in Wilmington, North Carolina, of disease, likely malaria or tuberculosis. Local black newspapers, including the *Christian Recorder*, sadly noted his exemplary character and willingness to sacrifice. (Donald McMurray.)

Located on Washington Street in Philadelphia, the Union Refreshment Volunteer Saloon was frequented by Camp William Penn's soldiers. Camp commander Col. Louis Wagner and men of the 6th and 8th Regiments were served there on October 3, 1863, according to the *Christian Recorder*, noting that the facility served black and white soldiers with "no difference." (United States Sanitary Commission Records, Manuscripts and Archives Division, the New York Public Library; Astor, Lenox, and Tilden Foundations.)

The Battle of New Market Heights or Chaffin's Farm in Virginia on September 29 to 30, 1864, involved several Camp William Penn USCT regiments, including the 6th and 22nd. Several members of the 6th, including Sgt. Thomas Hawkins, Sgt. Alexander Kelly, and Lt. Nathan H. Edgerton, performed meritoriously to earn the Medal of Honor while protecting and saving the regimental flags and colors. (Library of Congress.)

This first of a two-part 1864 carte de visite photograph features African American children in ragged clothing who were rescued by Capt. Girard Riley, 6th Regiment United States Colored Infantry (USCI), from a Mathews County, Virginia, slave owner named Thomas White. The boy and girl are described as "Virginia slave children rescued by colored troops—as we found them" and were sent by Riley to Philadelphia to be educated at the Orphanage for Colored Children via the Society of Friends. (Virginia Historical Society.)

In this second photograph, "As they are now," the same rescued children now appear healthy and groomed. The mother of the children was described as having been sold at auction on February 13, 1864, then "beaten and branded for being kind to Union Soldiers." As she departed to Virginia the mother reportedly prayed, "O, God send the Yankees to take my children away." (Virginia Historical Society.)

Philadelphia area abolitionists supported orphanages for black children. Pictured above are infants and their caretakers, black women in dresses, posing in this rare photograph of the Orphanage for Colored Children in Philadelphia. The burning of such facilities by white mobs in Philadelphia and New York City before and during the Civil War likely rallied more black men to the Union's cause. (Friends Historical Library at Swarthmore College.)

Nicholas Biddle has been unofficially associated Pennsylvania's Washington Artillerists and likely knew soldiers who trained at Camp William Penn. The Pottsville, Pa. resident is historically known as the first person wounded in the Civil War after receiving a head injury during the Baltimore Riots of April 1861 as he marched with the group that became part of Pennsylvania's 48th Infantry. An ex-slave like many Camp WIlliam Penn soldiers, Biddle, served as an aide to commanding officer Captain James Wren, despite being 65 years old at the start of the war. (U.S. Army Military History Institute.)

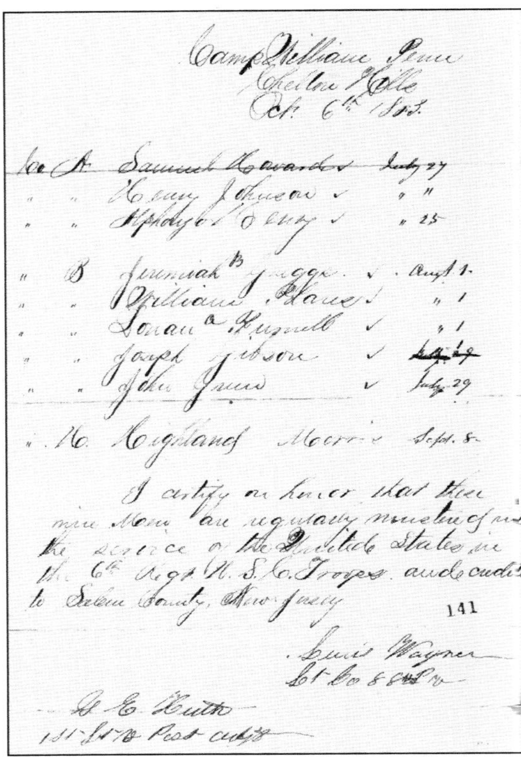

Camp William Penn
Chelten Hills
Oct. 6th 1863.

Co.	A	Samuel Howard ✓		July 27
"	"	Henry Johnson ✓		" "
"	"	Alphodges [illegible] ✓		" 25
"	B	Jeremiah B. Griggs	✓	Aug. 1
"	"	William Haws	✓	" 1
"	"	Lorenzo Russell	✓	" 1
"	"	Joseph Gibson	✓	[illegible]
"	"	John Jones	✓	July 29
"	K	Highland Moore	✓	Sept. 8

I certify on honor that these nine Men are regularly mustered into the service of the United States in the 6th Regt. U. S. C. Troops and credited to Salem County, New Jersey

141

Louis Wagner
Lt Co 88th Pa

G. E. Keith
1st Lt [illegible] Post Adjt

Pvt. Samuel Howard belonged to the 6th Regiment USCT, from which three soldiers earned the Medal of Honor for meritorious action during the September 1864 Battle of New Market Heights or Chaffin's Farm. Hailing from Salem County, New Jersey, Howard's name appears first on a mustering-in letter signed by the camp's commander, Louis Wagner, on October 6, 1863. He was mustered in on July 27, 1863, into Company K. (New Jersey State Archives.)

African American Medal of Honor recipients pictured here include a couple from the 6th Regiment USCT. Alexander Kelly is pictured on the fourth row, second from the left. Thomas R. Hawkins is shown in the third row, also second from the left. The 15 African American soldiers and sailors include, from left to right, (first row) Robert A. Penn, Milton M. Holland, and Sgt. John Lawson; (second row) Sgt. John Denny, Cpl. Isaiah Mays, Powhatan Beaty, and Sgt. Brent Woods; (third row) Sgt. William Carney, Thomas R. Hawkins, Dennis Bell, and James H. Harris; (fourth row) Sgt. Thomas Shaw, Sgt. Alexander Kelly, Pvt. James Daniel Garner, and Christian Fleetwood. (Library of Congress.)

Sgt. Alexander Kelly was in Company F of the 6th Regiment USCT, receiving the Medal of Honor for heroic deeds at the Battle of New Market Heights or Chaffin's Farm in Virginia in September 1864. He is credited with grabbing the regiment's flag after its holder, Lt. Nathan H. Edgerton of the 6th, was wounded. Kelly's name appears on the African American Civil War Memorial in Washington, D.C. (Library of Congress.)

Sgt. Maj. Thomas R. Hawkins of the 6th Regiment USCT's Company C also earned the Medal of Honor for saving the regimental colors during the Battle of New Market Heights or Chaffin's Farm in Virginia in late September 1864. His name appears on the African American Memorial in Washington, D.C. (Library of Congress.)

Capt. Nathan H. Edgerton seized the colors of the 6th Regiment USCT during the Battle of New Market Heights or Chaffin's Farm after the holder, Lt. Frederick Meyer, was shot through the heart during the raging battle. However, Edgerton was also shot and began bleeding profusely when the flag was seized by Sgt. Alexander Kelly of Company F. (Library of Congress.)

Col. John W. Ames was originally mustered into service on May 14, 1861, and boldly led the 6th Regiment USCT from Camp William Penn into one of the bloodiest engagements of the war, Chaffin's Farm in Virginia, on September 29, 1864. On that day he was wounded during battle, also known as New Market Heights. He had been promoted from captain of the 11th Infantry and after being injured ascended to brigadier general. (U.S. Army Military History Institute.)

Capt. George E. Heath mustered into service on August 24, 1863, and joined the 6th Regiment USCT at Camp William Penn. He was promoted from first lieutenant to captain of Company D on March 28, 1865. He was mustered out with his company on September 20, 1865. (U.S. Army Military History Institute.)

On October 5, 1863, 1st Lt. John B. Johnson mustered into service and became affiliated with the 6th Regiment USCT at Camp William Penn. He was promoted from second lieutenant on February 15, 1865. He was discharged by special order on January 26, 1865, due to wounds received at New Market Heights, Virginia, on September 29, 1864. (U.S. Army Military History Institute.)

On October 8, 1863, 1st Lt. Nathaniel N. Hubbard mustered into service. He joined Company B of the 6th Regiment USCT at Camp William Penn. He was wounded at New Market Heights, Virginia, on September 29, 1864. He was discharged on surgeon's certificate on March 3, 1865. (U.S. Army Military History Institute.)

November 2, 1864, was the date 1st Lt. Morton P. Kellogg was mustered into service. He joined Company C of the 25th Regiment USCT at Camp William Penn. He was discharged on September 20, 1865. (U.S. Army Military History Institute.)

Addison Palmer mustered into the 6th Regiment USCT of Camp William Penn on September 5, 1863, as a private, likely meaning that he was of mixed ancestry that included being African American and/or American Indian. He was promoted to sergeant on July 20, 1865, and mustered out with his company on September 20, 1865. He is listed on the African American Civil War Memorial in Washington, D.C. (U.S. Army Military History Institute.)

Capt. John McMurray led Company D of the 6th Regiment USCT that saw major action in New Market Heights, Virginia, in September 1864, when several of the regiment's members earned the Medal of Honor while protecting the colors. Mustered into service on September 24, 1863, McMurray became a brevet major on April 15, 1865, and major on September 26, 1865. (U.S. Army Military History Institute.)

Capt. Robert B. Beath was originally mustered into service on September 5, 1861. He joined the 6th USCT's Company A after being promoted to captain on August 29, 1863. He was wounded and loss a leg at the Battle of New Market Heights or Chaffin's Farm in Virginia on September 29, 1864, and was commissioned a lieutenant colonel on September 26, 1865, about the time that he was mustered out with his regiment. (U.S. Army Military History Institute.)

Joseph Gouldring was a lieutenant of the 6th USCT that saw major action at the Battle of New Market Heights or Chaffin's Farm in Virginia. Several soldiers earned the Medal of Honor for saving the regiment's colors, including two black recruits and a white officer. Gouldring is likely wearing Grand Army of the Republic (GAR) attire and distinguished service medals. (National Archives.)

On September 2, 1863, 2nd Lt. Eber C. Pratt was originally mustered in. He joined the 6th Regiment USCT. He most likely trained at the Free Military School for Applicants to Command Colored Troops in Philadelphia. Pratt died at Fortress Monroe, Virginia, in December 1864 of wounds he received at New Market Heights on September 29, 1864. (U.S. Army Military History Institute.)

Sgt. William Sterling joined Company C of the 6th USCT. This regiment organized at Camp William Penn from July 28 to September 12, 1863. The troops moved from Philadelphia to Fort Monroe, Virginia, on October 14. This infantry mustered out on September 20, 1865. He's buried at the Philadelphia National Cemetery. (Donald Scott Jr.)

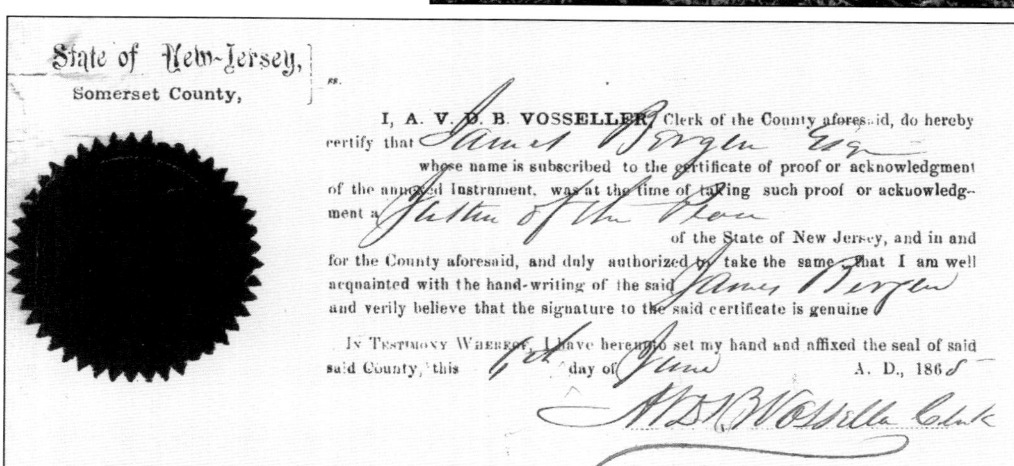

State of New-Jersey, Somerset County, ss.

I, A. V. D. B. VOSSELLER, Clerk of the County aforesaid, do hereby certify that James Bergen Esq whose name is subscribed to the certificate of proof or acknowledgment of the annexed Instrument, was at the time of taking such proof or acknowledgment a Justice of the Peace of the State of New Jersey, and in and for the County aforesaid, and duly authorized to take the same. That I am well acquainted with the hand-writing of the said James Bergen and verily believe that the signature to the said certificate is genuine.

In Testimony Whereof, I have hereunto set my hand and affixed the seal of said County, this 6th day of June A. D., 1865

A. V. D. B. Vosseller Clerk

James Tenbrook of Somerville, New Jersey, was mustered in as a private of the 8th USCT at Camp William Penn, Company I, on November 16, 1863. His wife, Rebecca, apparently could not write because she signed an affidavit when applying for state funds for her husband's service with an X. Tenbrook's muster form was signed on December 11, 1863, shortly before the regiment arrived at Hilton Head, South Carolina, on January 16, 1864. (New Jersey State Archives.)

Col. Charles W. Fribley mustered into service on October 9, 1861, and joined the 8th Regiment at Camp William Penn. He was promoted from captain of Company F of the 84th Regiment Pennsylvania Volunteers on November 23, 1863. However, he was killed at Olustee, Florida, on February 20, 1864. (U.S. Army Military History Institute.)

First Lt. J. Francis Jenness was promoted from second lieutenant of the 8th USCT's Company G on April 1, 1865, and joined Company B. The 8th suffered very heavy losses during the Battle of Olustee in Florida in February 1864. George E. Wagner, the brother of the camp's commander, Louis Wagner, was wounded at Olustee. Jenness and the regiment also saw major action in Virginia. (U.S. Army Military History Institute.)

Quartermaster Oliver W. Norton mustered into service on December 31, 1863. He joined the 8th Regiment USCT at Camp William Penn. He was promoted from first lieutenant of Company K on August 30, 1865, to quartermaster on August 30, 1865. Norton's written accounts of the 8th Regiment's heavy losses when combating hardened Confederate troops during the Battle of Olustee in Florida have been recounted in various historical sources. (U.S. Army Military History Institute.)

This obverse side of the 22nd Regiment's flag displays black artist David Bowser's dramatic flair with a black soldier bayoneting a Confederate officer. Such a depiction was novel in itself since it legally portrays a black soldier killing a white man. Many of the 22nd recruits hailed from New Jersey. The regiment fought in several major battles, as well as led Lincoln's funeral procession in Washington, D.C., on April 20, 1865. (Library of Congress.)

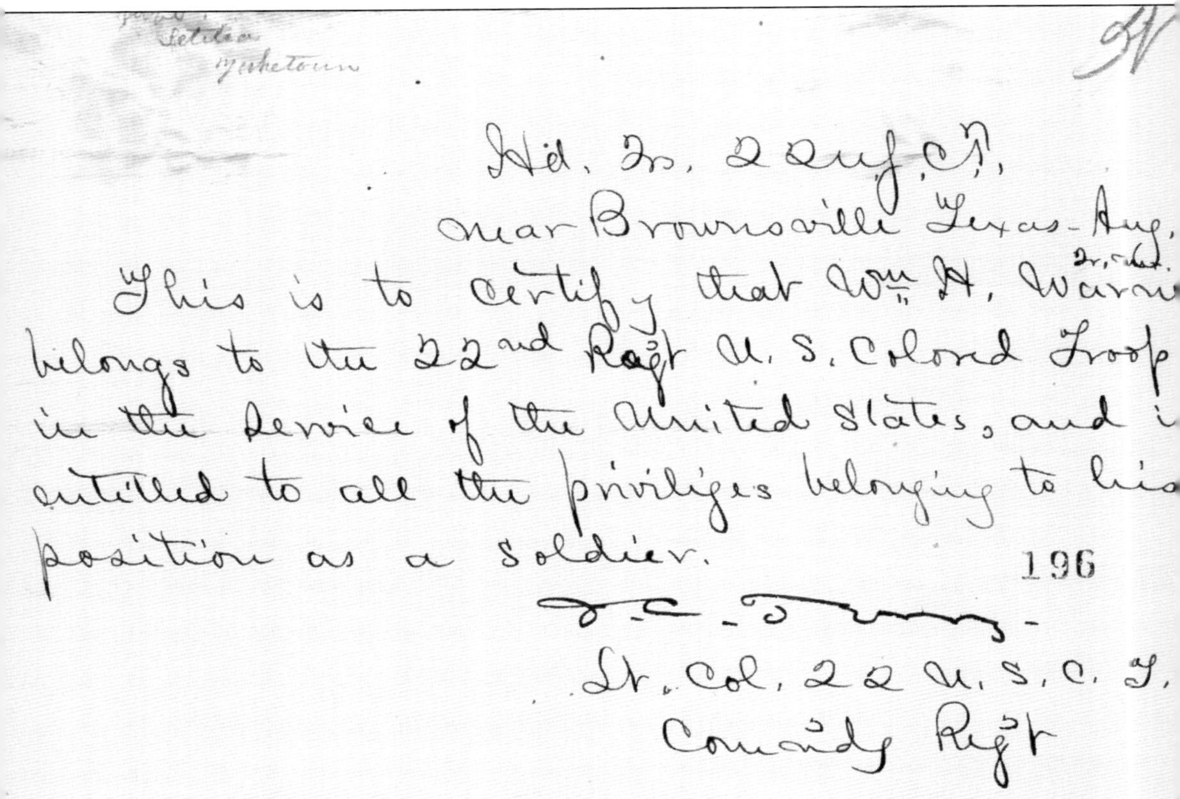

Hd. Qrs. 22 Inf. C.T.
near Brownsville Texas - Aug.
This is to certify that Wm. H. Warner
belongs to the 22nd Regt U. S. Colord Troops
in the Service of the United States, and is
entitled to all the priviliges belonging to his
position as a soldier.
196

Lt. Col. 22 U. S. C. T.
Comdg Regt

Salem, New Jersey, resident William H. Warner signed on as a private in the 22nd Regiment USCT's Company A on December 7, 1863. There is an indication that he rose to the rank of sergeant and then quartermaster sergeant. He is recognized on the African American Civil War Memorial in Washington, D.C. The 22nd was ordered to Yorktown, Virginia, in January 1864 after it was organized at Camp William Penn from January 10 through the 29. Warner and the 22nd participated in major battles and suffered notable losses at such places as Chaffin's Farm and Fair Oaks before participating in Lincoln's funeral and pursuing the president's assassins. The regiment was mustered out in Brownsville, Texas, on October 16, 1865. (New Jersey State Archives.)

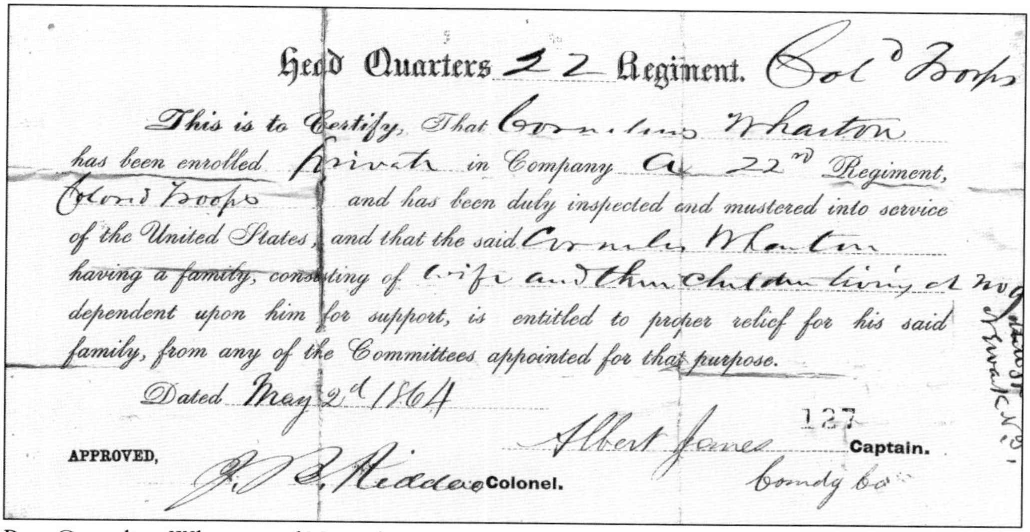

Head Quarters 22 Regiment. Col^d Troops

This is to Certify, That Cornelius Wharton has been enrolled Private in Company A 22nd Regiment, Colored Troops and has been duly inspected and mustered into service of the United States, and that the said Cornelius Wharton having a family, consisting of wife and three children living at No [illegible] Newark N.J. dependent upon him for support, is entitled to proper relief for his said family, from any of the Committees appointed for that purpose.

Dated May 2^d 1864

127

APPROVED, [illegible] Colonel.

Albert Janes Captain. Comdg Co

Pvt. Cornelius Wharton of Newark, New Jersey, belonged to the very active 22nd Regiment's Company A and was married with three children during the war. His wife and children were living in Newark when Wharton's captain signed a certificate in May 1864 verifying the private's service to the United States. The document noted that Wharton's family was "dependent upon him for support" and "entitled to proper relief." (New Jersey State Archives.)

SIEGE OF PETERSBURG—THE COLORED INFANTRY BRINGING IN CAPTURED GUNS AMID CHEERS OF THE OHIO TROOPS.
FROM A SKETCH BY OUR SPECIAL ARTIST, E. F. MULLEN.

When the colored troops found themselves within the works of the enemy no words could paint their delight. Numbers of them kissed the guns [...] had captured with extravagant satisfaction, and a feverish anxiety was manifested to get ahead and charge some more of the Confederate works. [...]umber of the colored troops were wounded and a few killed in the first charge. A large crowd congregated, with looks of unutterable admiration, [...]t Sergeant Richardson and Corporal Wobey, of the Twenty-second United States colored regiment, who had carried the colors of their regiment and [...] the first men in the works. Our artist gives a sketch of this gallant action.

438

The "Siege of Petersburg—The Colored Infantry Bringing in Captured Guns amid cheers of the Ohio Troops" was a newspaper drawing illustrated probably in 1865 by E. F. Mullin. It shows the crowd's admiration of the 22nd USCT color bearers—Sgt. Edward Richardson and Corp. James Wobey. An account describes the "gallant action" of the black troops who "kissed the ground they had captured with extravagant satisfaction." (Virginia Historical Society.)

The fighting at Petersburg, Virginia, of the 22nd USCT from Camp William Penn was recorded in this painting by artist Andre Castaigne and is part of the West Point Museum Collections at the U.S. military academy. Organized at Philadelphia from January 10 through 29, 1864, the regiment started service near Yorktown, Virginia, and participated in action at Chaffin's Farm and Fair Oaks in Virginia. (Picture Collection, the Branch Libraries, the New York City Public Library, Astor, Lenox, and Tilden Foundations.)

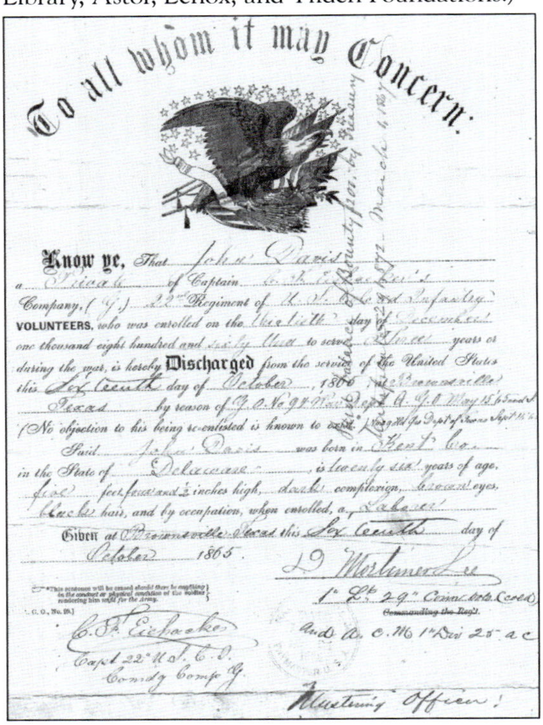

To all whom it may Concern:

Know ye, That John Davis
a Private of Captain C. F. Eichacker's
Company, (G) 22nd Regiment of U. S. Col'd Infantry
VOLUNTEERS, who was enrolled on the thirtieth day of December
one thousand eight hundred and sixty three to serve three years or
during the war, is hereby Discharged from the service of the United States
this Sixteenth day of October, 1865, at Brownsville
Texas by reason of G. O. No 94 War Dept A. G. O May 15 1865
(No objection to his being re-enlisted is known to exist.)*
Said John Davis was born in Kent Co.
in the State of Delaware, is twenty six years of age,
five feet four and ½ inches high, dark complexion, brown eyes,
black hair, and by occupation, when enrolled, a Laborer
Given at Brownsville Texas this Sixteenth day of
October 1865.

D. Mortimer Lee
1st Lt. 29th Conn. Vols. (Col'd)
~~Commanding the Reg't.~~
and A. C. M. 1st Div 25 A. C.

*This sentence will be erased should there be anything in the conduct or physical condition of the soldier rendering him unfit for the Army.

C. F. Eichacker
Capt 22 U. S. C. T.
Comdg Comp G.

Mustering Officer!

Pvt. John Davis, born in Kent County, Delaware, joined the 22nd USCT's Company G and lived in New Jersey's Camden County. Mustered in at age 26, his stature was small and complexion "dark." Similar to many USCT soldiers, he was classified as a laborer at first but likely saw action as the war heated up. The 22nd was one of the camp's most active regiments. (Courtesy New Jersey State Archives.)

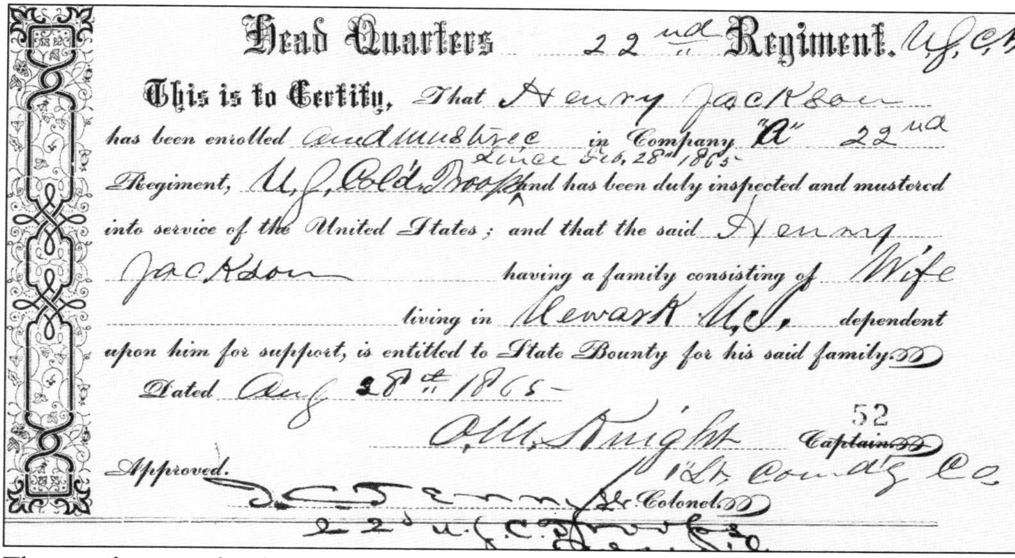

Head Quarters 22nd Regiment. U.S.C.T.

This is to Certify, That Henry Jackson has been enrolled and mustered in Company "A" 22nd Regiment, U.S. Cold Troops since Feb. 28th 1865 and has been duly inspected and mustered into service of the United States; and that the said Henry Jackson having a family consisting of Wife living in Newark N.J., dependent upon him for support, is entitled to State Bounty for his said family.

Dated Aug 28th 1865

52

O.M. Knight Captain
1st Lt. Comdg Co.

Approved.

[illegible] Lt. Colonel
22nd U.S.C.T. [illegible]

This certificate verifies that Henry Jackson was a member of the 22nd USCT's Company A. He apparently was mustered in early in 1865 and served about half a year when the form was filled out on August 28, 1865. The Newark, New Jersey, resident, according to the document, sought the state bounty to help support his wife, who is unnamed on the form that originated at the "Head Quarters" of the 22nd Regiment USCT. (New Jersey Archives.)

George W. Keyes, a private in Company F of the 22nd USCT, was a member of GAR Post 139 in Scranton following the Civil War. Keyes likely saw action in Virginia, including at the Battle of New Market Heights or Chaffin's Farm on September 29, 1864. (U.S. Army Military History Institute.)

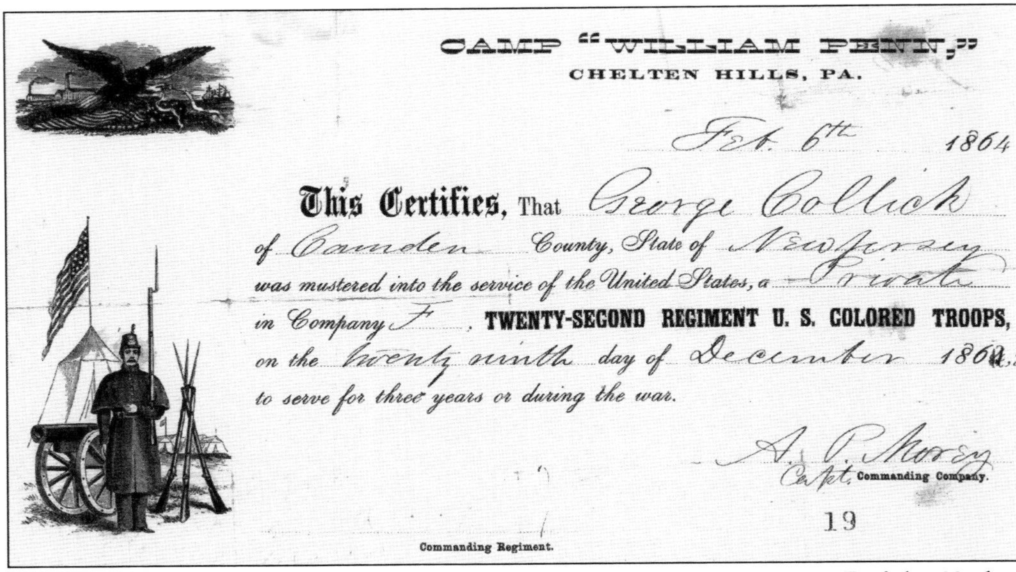
CAMP "WILLIAM PENN,"
CHELTEN HILLS, PA.

Feb. 6th 1864

This Certifies, That George Collick
of Camden County, State of New Jersey
was mustered into the service of the United States, a Private
in Company F, TWENTY-SECOND REGIMENT U. S. COLORED TROOPS,
on the twenty ninth day of December 1863,
to serve for three years or during the war.

A. P. Morey
Capt. Commanding Company.

19

Commanding Regiment.

Hailing from Camden, New Jersey, George Collick mustered into Company F of the 22nd on December 29, 1863, as a private. Collick saw action in Virginia, Washington, D.C. (where Pres. Abraham Lincoln's assassins were pursued by the 22nd), and in Texas at the end of the war. Duty for Collick and his fellow men was not easy since the 22nd lost 70 enlisted men and several officers in combat. Almost 150 died of disease. (New Jersey State Archives.)

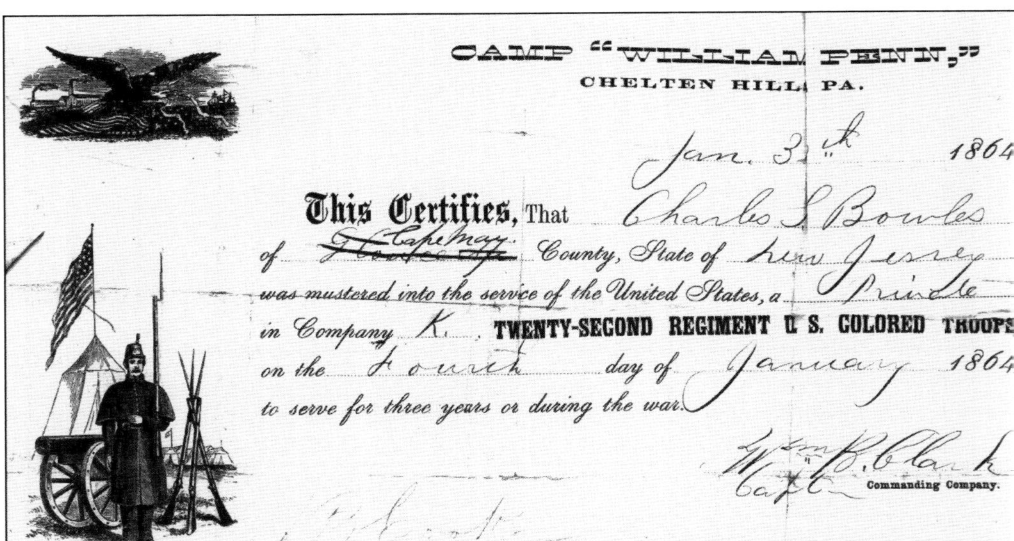
CAMP "WILLIAM PENN,"
CHELTEN HILLS, PA.

Jan. 31th 1864

This Certifies, That Charles S Bowles
of Cape May County, State of New Jersey
was mustered into the service of the United States, a Private
in Company K, TWENTY-SECOND REGIMENT U. S. COLORED TROOPS,
on the Fourth day of January 1864,
to serve for three years or during the war.

Wm B. Clark
Capt. Commanding Company.

Charles S. Bowles of the 22nd USCT's Company K mustered in as a private on January 4, 1864. Bowles hailed from Cape May, New Jersey. The 22nd saw much action while attached to U.S. forces in Virginia and North Carolina. Bowles and the regiment also fought in Virginia and pursued Lincoln's assassins before serving in the Rio Grande until October 1865. (New Jersey State Archives.)

Sgt. Edward Richardson, an ex-slave and native of Cecil County Maryland, was a member of the 22nd USCT. Richardson and his wife Fannie Sturges were respected citizens of South Jersey for many years, with Richardson serving as the color bearer during some of the fiercest combats of the war, including at Petersburg. His war record was described as "a most enviable one." He married Sturges in 1886, and the couple had 10 children, many of them encouraged to receive college degrees from a father who learned to read and write after running away to a family (the Lippincotts) that would allow him to study. Although his mother had left him as a child via the Underground Railroad, Richardson's determination, intelligence, and enterprise allowed him to accrue wealth and property. He also became an accomplished musician and member of the local school board in Woodstown. (U.S. Army Military History Institute.)

Capt. Jacob F. Force led the 22nd USCT's Company H. Force had been promoted from the rank of lieutenant, according to National Park Service records. He is listed in Washington, D.C., on the African American Civil War Memorial. (U.S. Army Military History Institute.)

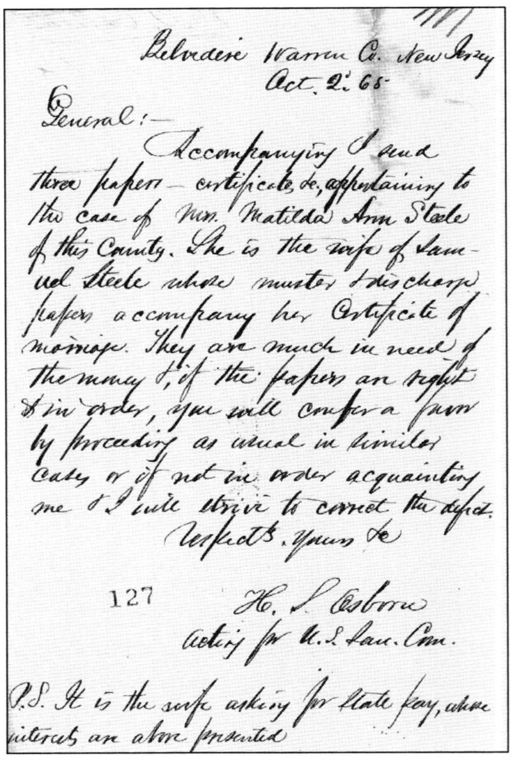

Belvedere Warren Co. New Jersey
Oct. 2: 65

General:—

Accompanying I send three papers — certificate &c, appertaining to the case of Mrs. Matilda Ann Steele of this County. She is the wife of Samuel Steele whose muster & discharge papers accompany her Certificate of marriage. They are much in need of the money & if the papers are right & in order, you will confer a favor by proceeding as usual in similar cases or if not in order acquainting me & I will strive to correct the defect.

Respects. Yours &c

127 H. S. Osborne
Acting for U.S. San. Com.

P.S. It is the wife asking for State pay, whose interests are above presented

Pvt. Samuel Steele's wife, Matilda Ann, was the focus of an October 1865 letter certifying that the couple was married and that he had fought in Company I of the 22nd USCT from Camp William Penn. Steele and other black soldiers often had to get such documents in order to receive financial support for their family. She was "much in need of the money," the letter indicates. (New Jersey State Archives.)

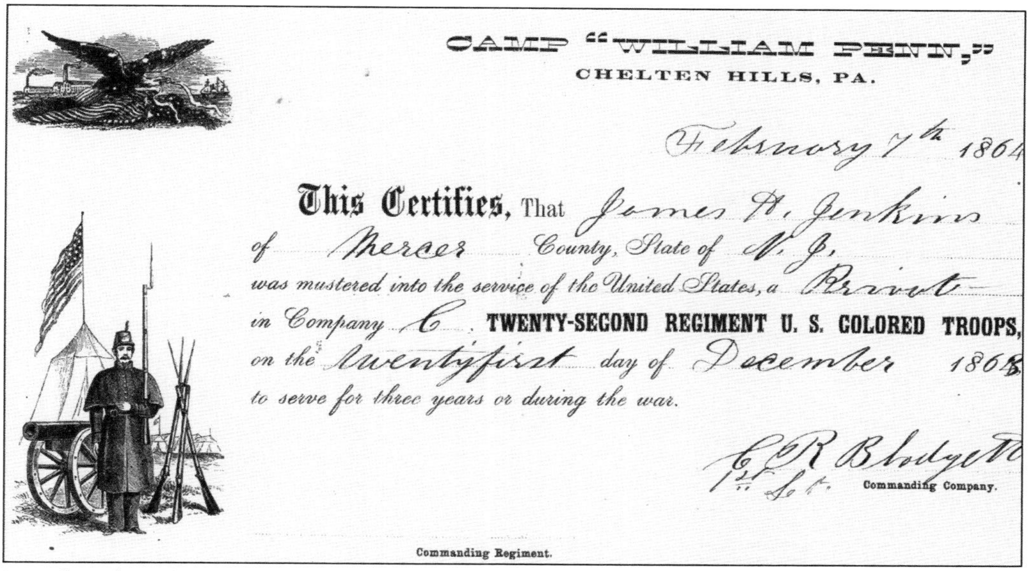

CAMP "WILLIAM PENN,"
CHELTEN HILLS, PA.

February 7th 1864

This Certifies, That James H. Jenkins of Mercer County, State of N. J. was mustered into the service of the United States, a Private in Company C TWENTY-SECOND REGIMENT U. S. COLORED TROOPS, on the Twentyfirst day of December 1863 to serve for three years or during the war.

C. R. Blodgett 1st Lt. Commanding Company.

Commanding Regiment.

Listed on the African American Civil War Memorial in Washington, D.C., Pvt. James H. Jenkins was mustered into Company C of the 22nd USCT at Camp William Penn on December 21, 1863. The Mercer County, New Jersey, native's mustering-in form features the Camp William Penn insignia at the upper left. The 22nd was one of the most active units from the Philadelphia area camp. (New Jersey State Archives.)

Cpl. Alfred Schanck, buried at the Philadelphia National Cemetery, joined Company D of the 22nd Regiment USCT. He participated in the Petersburg assault as well as the engagement at New Market Heights. (Donald Scott Jr.)

Benjamin Furgeson, a private, served in Company C of the 22nd Regiment USCT. The regiment participated in the Petersburg assault as well as the engagement at New Market Heights. Furgeson is buried at the Philadelphia National Cemetery. (Donald Scott Jr.)

George Burr, likely a private and resting at the Philadelphia National Cemetery, served in Company C of the 22nd USCT, organized at Camp William Penn. These troops also participated in the engagement at New Market Heights as well as the Petersburg assault. (Donald Scott Jr.)

The 24th USCT was organized at Camp William Penn from January to March 1865. During a flag presentation ceremony in April, black activist and scholar Octavius V. Catto gave a rousing speech. Also, the Underground Railroad's supreme conductor Harriet Tubman delivered a speech to the men at Camp William Penn, despite a $40,000 bounty being placed on her head for helping numerous slaves to escape north. (Library Company of Philadelphia.)

This image of Pvt. John Merryweather of the 24th Regiment's Company C was taken while he was a member of the GAR Post 139 of Scranton after the war. GAR units began to accept black Civil War veterans during and after the Reconstruction period of the late 1800s and as racist Jim Crow (segregation) policies began to expand across the country. Primarily black GAR posts were also established. (U.S. Army Military History Institute.)

This unidentified soldier was a member of the 24th Regiment USCT of Camp William Penn. The image was captured not long after the Civil War. The ex-soldier's attire likely reflects a degree of financial security as he intently gazes at the camera. (U.S. Army Military History Institute.)

Lloyd F. A. Watts, a Gettysburg native, of the 24th USCT trained at Camp William Penn in the spring of 1865 as the war wound down. Eventually rising to the rank of sergeant, Watts guarded Confederate prisoners at Point Lookout in Maryland. In a letter to his wife, he noted that there were "twenty-five thousand Rebels [*sic*] prisoners here we have to guard. It takes one hundred men for guard duty." (Adams County Historical Society.)

Pvt. Thomas Lancaster, at rest in the Philadelphia National Cemetery, served in Company H of the 24th Regiment USCT. This regiment was organized at Camp William Penn from January 30 to March 30, 1865. The troops were mustered out October 1, 1865. (Donald Scott Jr.)

The 25th Regiment USCT's flag, designed by David Bowser, shows Lady Liberty giving a recently liberated black slave, with broken shackles on the ground, a bayoneted rifle. The motto on top reads, "Strike for God and liberty." The 25th served in Beaufort, North Carolina, New Orleans, and several major Florida battles. The regiment was mustered out on December 6, 1865. (Library of Congress.)

The 25th USCT stands at center camp in full dress as two officers on horseback pose in the foreground with onlookers viewing from buildings' porches in their fine attire. An officer on foot stands at attention with his men, many of them ex-slaves, gazing forward and ready for battle. Organized at Camp William Penn from January 3 to February 12, 1864, when this photograph was likely shot, the 25th was ordered to Beaufort, North Carolina, on the way to New Orleans when its transport, the steamer *Suwahnee*, began to take on water on March 15, 1864. After defending Beaufort's harbor, it served or saw action in New Orleans and Florida. The men were mustered out in December 1865. (National Archives.)

Camp William Penn's commander Louis Wagner enlisted Pvt. Thomas Crawford into Company D of the 25th USCT, according to a letter from the "Chief Mustering and Disbursing Office" of September 5, 1866. The note was apparently written to correct a mistake that gave some kind of credit, likely for monetary payment or for time served in the army. (New Jersey State Archives.)

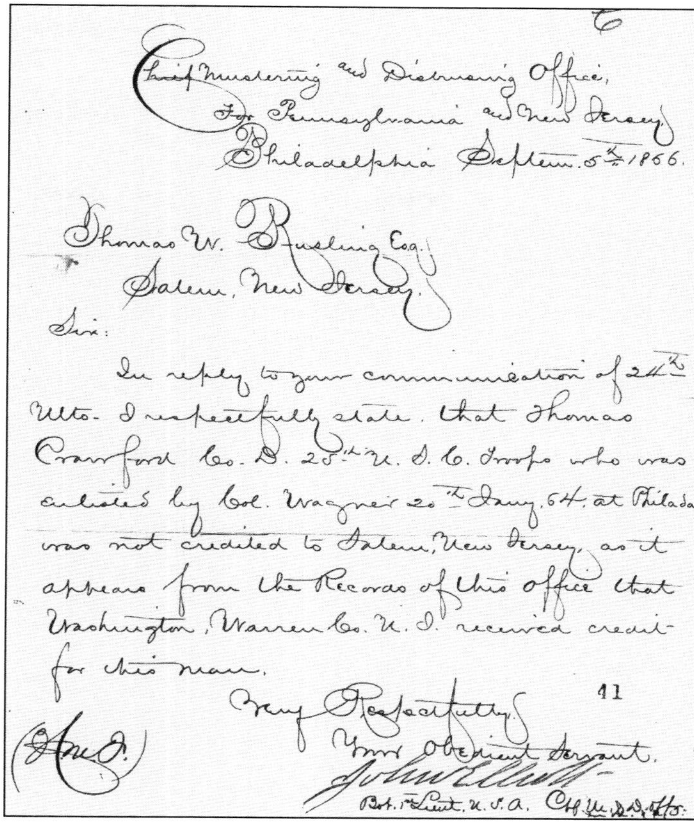

6

Chief Mustering and Disbursing Office,
For Pennsylvania and New Jersey
Philadelphia Septem. 5th 1866.

Thomas W. Rusling Esq.
Salem, New Jersey.

Sir:

In reply to your communication of 24th Ulto. I respectfully state that Thomas Crawford Co. D. 25th U.S.C. Troops who was enlisted by Col. Wagner 20th Jany. 64. at Philada. was not credited to Salem, New Jersey, as it appears from the Records of this Office that Washington, Warren Co. N.J. received credit for this man.

41

Very Respectfully
Your Obedient Servant.
[illegible]
Bvt. 1st Lieut. U.S.A. Ch. M. & D. Ofs.

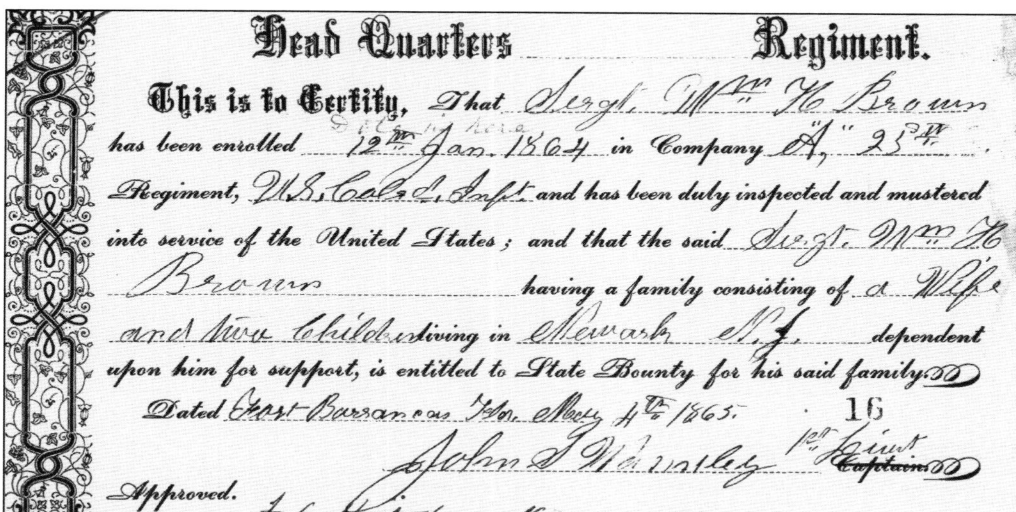

Head Quarters ____ Regiment.

This is to Certify, That Sergt. Wm H. Brown has been enrolled 12th Jan. 1864 in Company "A," 25th Regiment, U.S. Col'd. Inft. and has been duly inspected and mustered into service of the United States; and that the said Sergt. Wm H. Brown having a family consisting of a Wife and two Children living in Newark N.J. dependent upon him for support, is entitled to State Bounty for his said family.

Dated Fort Barrancas Fla. May 4th 1865. 16

John S. Wamsley 1st Lieut ~~Captain~~

Approved. F. L. Hitchcock Colonel.

Sgt. William H. Brown of Newark, New Jersey, was mustered into Company A of the 25th USCT on January 12, 1864. As his Camp William Penn muster form says, he was mandated to "serve for three years or during the war." (New Jersey State Archives.)

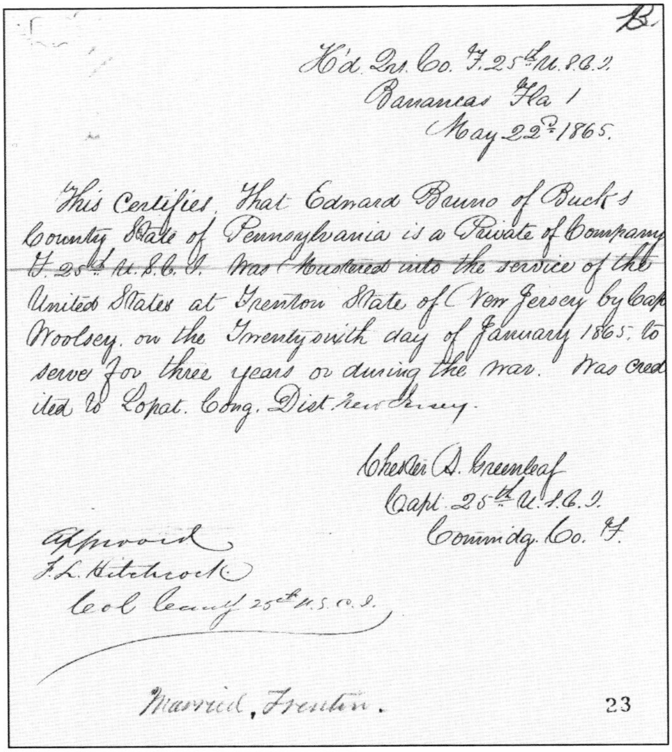

B

H'd Qrs. Co. F. 25th U.S.C.T.
Barrancas Fla
May 22nd 1865.

This Certifies, That Edward Bruno of Buck's County State of Pennsylvania is a Private of Company F. 25th U.S.C.T. Was Mustered into the service of the United States at Trenton State of New Jersey by Capt Woolsey, on the Twenty sixth day of January 1865, to serve for three years or during the war. Was Credited to [illegible] Cong. Dist. New Jersey.

Chester A. Greenleaf
Capt. 25th U.S.C.T.
Commdg. Co. F.

Approved
F. L. Hitchcock
Col Comdg 25th U.S.C.T.

Married, Trenton.

23

Edward Bruno, a private in Company K of the 25th USCT, was also known as Edward Brown, according to the Civil War Soldiers and Sailors System online data. Hailing from Buck's County, he was mustered in late January 1865. The May 22, 1865, letter was written by Capt. Chester Greenleaf of the 25th's Company F, likely in support of financial support or a pension, especially since the note also indicates that he was married. (New Jersey State Archives.)

Illustrated in *Harper's* pictorial history of the great rebellion, the "Negro" quarters of the Army of the James depicts camp life of the Camp William Penn African American troops embedded there at a crucial battle site of the war. (Picture Collection, the Branch Libraries, the New York Public Library, Astor, Lenox, and Tilden Foundations.)

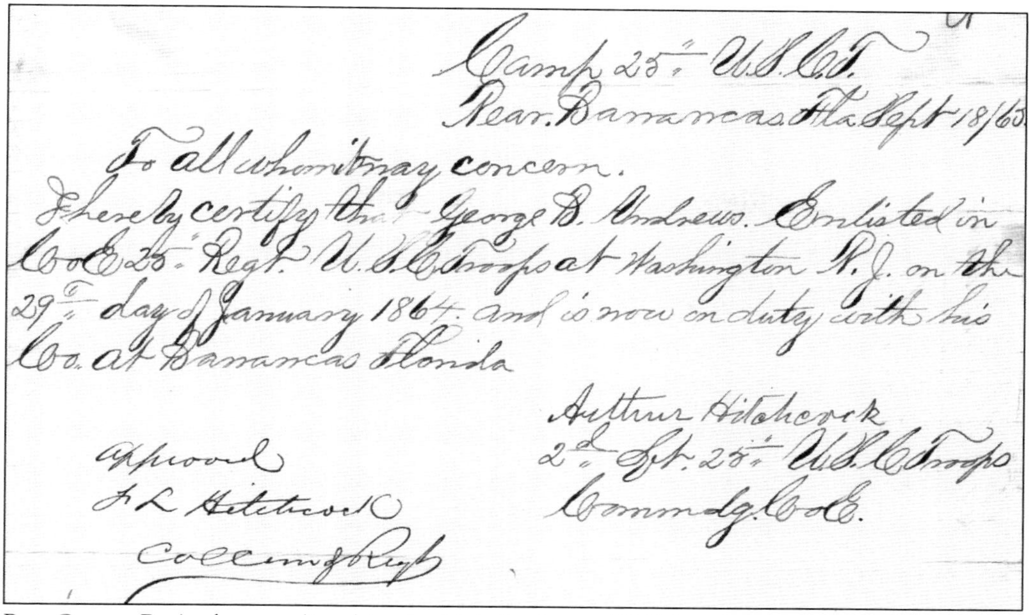

Camp 25th U.S.C.T.
Near Barrancas Fla Sept 18/65

To all whom it may concern.
I hereby certify that George B. Andrews. Enlisted in Co E 25th Regt. U.S.C. Troops at Washington N.J. on the 29th day of January 1864. and is now on duty with his Co. at Barrancas Florida

Arthur Hitchcock
2d Lt. 25th U.S.C. Troops
Commdg. Co E.

Approved
F L Hitchcock
Col Comdg Regt

Pvt. George B. Andrews enlisted in the 25th Regiment USCT on January 29, 1864, according to a letter written by his commanding officer, 2nd Lt. Arthur Hitchcock, while they were both serving in Barrancas, Florida. Andrews and his fellow black soldiers participated in garrison duty. Andrews and his comrades stopped in Beaufort, North Carolina, before continuing to New Orleans after their transporting steamship sprang a leak. (New Jersey State Archives.)

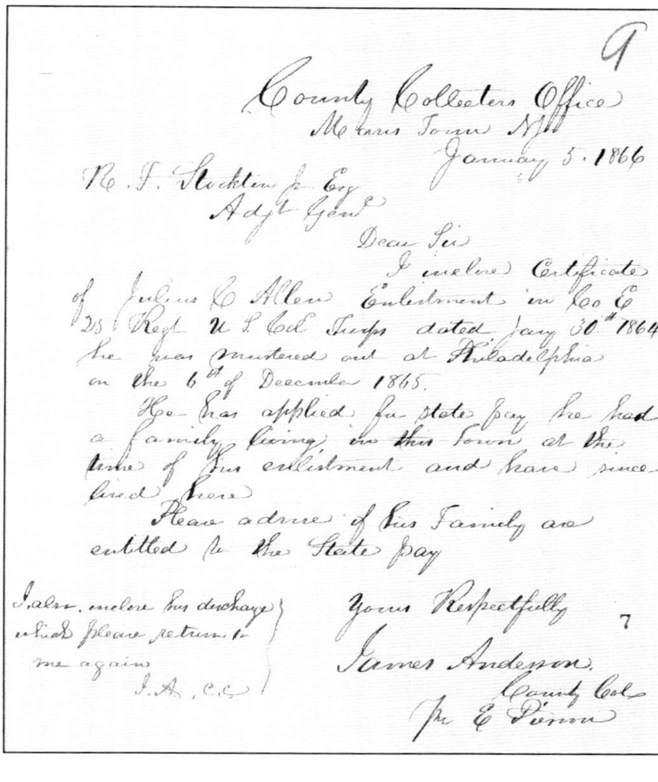

9

County Collectors Office
Morris Town NJ
January 5. 1866

R. F. Stockton Jr Esq
Adjt Genl

Dear Sir
I enclose Certificate of Julius C Allen Enlistment in Co E 25 Regt U S Col Troops dated Jany 30th 1864 he was mustered out at Philadelphia on the 6th of December 1865.
He has applied for state pay he had a family living in this town at the time of his enlistment and have since lived here
Please advise if his Family are entitled to the State pay

I also enclose his discharge which please return to me again J.A. C.C.

Yours Respectfully
James Anderson
County Col
pr E [illegible]

7

Julius C. Allen was mustered in on January 30, 1864, as a corporal in Company E of the 25th Regiment USCT. He was mustered out in Philadelphia almost a year later on December 6, 1865. James Anderson, a tax collector in New Jersey, wrote a January 5, 1866, letter to state officials after the war to try and get Allen and his family "state pay." (New Jersey State Archives.)

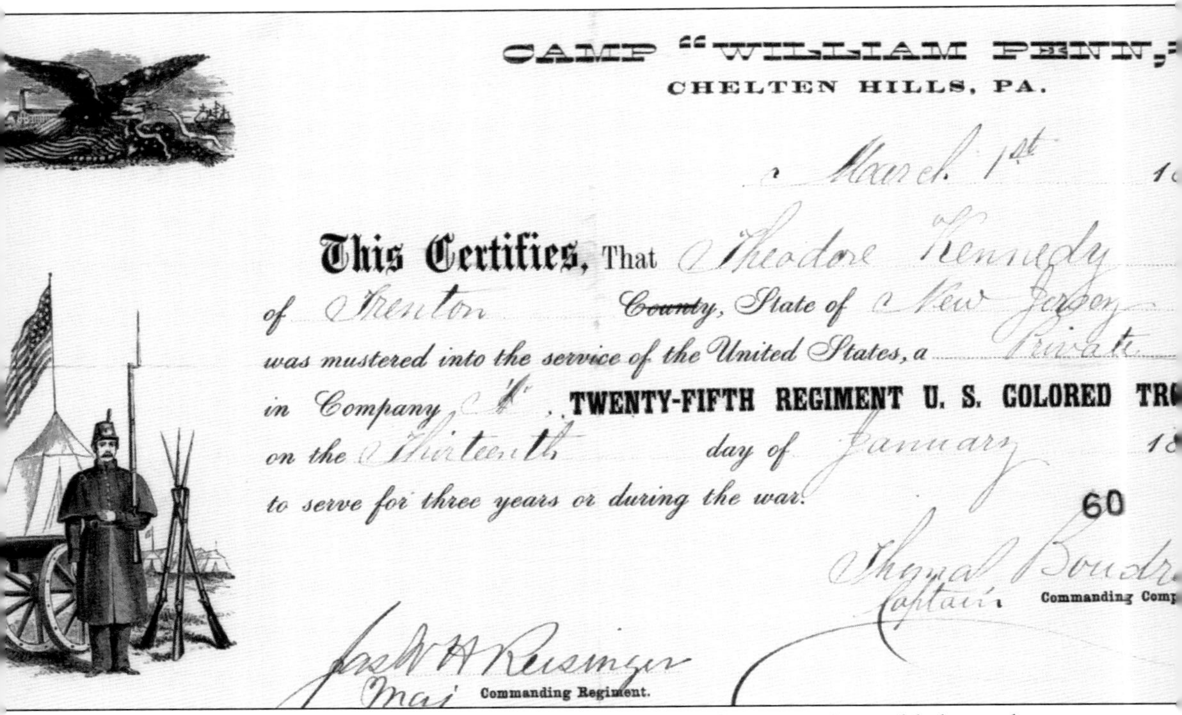

CAMP "WILLIAM PENN,"
CHELTEN HILLS, PA.

March 1st 18

This Certifies, That Theodore Kennedy
of Trenton ~~County~~, State of New Jersey
was mustered into the service of the United States, a Private
in Company A TWENTY-FIFTH REGIMENT U. S. COLORED TR
on the Thirteenth day of January 18
to serve for three years or during the war.

60

Thomas Boudr
Captain Commanding Comp

Jos W H Reisinger
Maj Commanding Regiment.

Pvt. Theodore Kennedy of the 25th Regiment USCT's Company A was likely on the steamer *Suwahnee* that was headed down the Atlantic coast toward the Gulf of Mexico when it sprang a leak in March 1864. Kennedy, a Trenton, New Jersey, native, temporarily helped with the defense of Beaufort, North Carolina, where the ship was repaired before moving on to New Orleans. (New Jersey State Archives.)

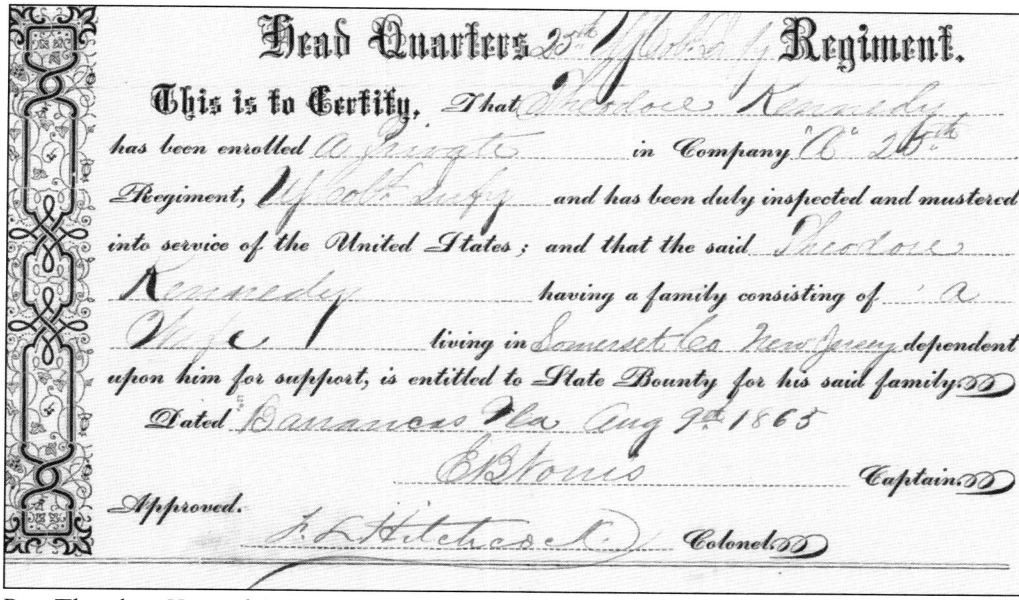

Head Quarters 25th U.S. Col'd Inf'y Regiment.

This is to Certify, That Theodore Kennedy has been enrolled a Private in Company "A" 25th Regiment, U.S. Col'd Inf'y and has been duly inspected and mustered into service of the United States; and that the said Theodore Kennedy having a family consisting of a Wife living in Somerset Co New Jersey dependent upon him for support, is entitled to State Bounty for his said family.

Dated Barrancas Fla Aug 9th 1865

E B Storrs Captain.

Approved.

F L Hitchcock Colonel.

Pvt. Theodore Kennedy's mustering certificate indicates that he was married. His wife lived in Somerset County, New Jersey, and was "dependent upon him for support." Serving in Florida at the time the certificate was issued, Kennedy was seeking "State Bounty for his said family." (New Jersey State Archives.)

On March 16, 1864, 1st Lt. George S. Mahaffy mustered into service. He joined Company I of the 25th Regiment USCT at Camp William Penn. He was mustered out with the rest of his company on December 6, 1865. (U.S. Army Military History Institute.)

On February 1, 1964, 1st Lt. Abbott A. Shattock mustered into service. He joined Company C of the 25th Regiment at Camp William Penn. He was promoted to captain of Company H on May 11, 1865. (U.S. Army Military History Institute.)

Col. Frederick L. Hitchcock mustered into service on January 27, 1864, and joined the 25th Regiment at Camp William Penn. He was promoted from lieutenant colonel on November 16, 1864. He mustered out of the regiment on December 6, 1865. (U.S. Army Military History Institute.)

Pvt. Perry Hall served in Camp William Penn's 25th USCT's Company C. In mid-March 1864, much of the regiment loaded on to a steamer that soon took on water caused by a leak off the coast of Beaufort, North Carolina. They helped to defend the town before Hall and the regiment continued to New Orleans and eventually saw duty in Florida. During the summer of 1865, scurvy struck and more than 150 died, with many suffering lifetime illness as a result. (Cicero Green.)

Appearing quite distinguished in this image, Hall and his fellow soldiers were mustered out at Camp Cadwalader in Philadelphia on December 6, 1865. He suffered throughout his life from physical problems due to his service. Today Perry Hall's descendant Cicero Green lives near the same community where Camp William Penn once stood. Green recovered the images from a relative as they were about to be discarded. (Cicero Green.)

Col. Frederick L. Hitchcock, destined to become a member of the GAR after the war, led the 25th USCT of Camp William Penn. The regiment was one of the most photographed of the camp, at least based on the number of images that survive today. (U.S. Army Military History Institute.)

Maj. Thomas Boudren mustered into service on January 21, 1864. He joined the 25th USCT at Camp William Penn. He was promoted from lieutenant colonel on November 16, 1864. He mustered out with the regiment on December 6, 1865. (U.S. Army Military History Institute.)

First lieutenant and assistant surgeon John J. M. Angier mustered into service on February 12, 1864. He mustered out of regiment on December 6, 1865. (U.S. Army Military History Institute.)

Capt. George N. Copp mustered into service on September 19, 1862. He joined Company B of the 25th Regiment USCT. He was promoted from private of Company B, 13th Regiment New Hampshire Volunteers, to first lieutenant on February 1, 1864. He was promoted to captain on May 11, 1865. He mustered out of company on December 6, 1865. (U.S. Army Military History Institute.)

These two black soldiers depicted in Ed Hamilton's *Spirit of Freedom* statue at the African American Civil War Memorial in Washington, D.C., seem to be shielding, but leading, a black woman and the infant she is holding. When Camp William Penn troops, such as the 8th USCT, fought in such places as Olustee, Florida, they would often rescue black slaves. (Donald Scott Sr.)

Capt. George N. Copp poses for a picture with his wife. The wives of officers occasionally traveled with or to their husbands. Spouses or partners of the Camp William Penn soldiers sometimes visited the camp, especially as spectators, on weekends. (U.S. Army Military History Institute.)

Poised for action and with their fingers on the triggers of rifles, these black soldiers depicted in Ed Hamilton's *Spirit of Freedom* statue at the African American Civil War Memorial in Washington, D.C., represent the readiness of soldiers from Camp William Penn on a Civil War battle's front line. (Donald Scott Sr.)

Charles P. Fisher mustered into service on January 30, 1864, originally joining Company A of the 25th Regiment at Camp William Penn as a lieutenant and rising to the rank of captain. He was earlier a corporal of the 34th Regiment Massachusetts Volunteers, Company K. (U.S. Army Military History Institute.)

On January 18, 1864, 2nd Lt. Charles M. Edgarton joined the 25th USCT's Company G. However, he died of an undisclosed cause in Philadelphia on March 28, 1864. Therefore, it is not likely that he traveled with the regiment by steamer to North Carolina on March 15, 1864. Yet, he probably trained at the Free Military School for Applicants to Command Colored Troops in Philadelphia. (U.S. Army Military History Institute.)

February 7, 1864, was the day that 1st Lt. Albert Henry was mustered into the 25th USCT's Company E. The regiment and Henry first landed by steamship in Beaufort, North Carolina, after the vessel sprang a leak on its way to New Orleans. The regiment later served in Florida and other locales. Henry resigned on July 7, 1865. (U.S. Army Military History Institute.)

On June 5, 1865, 1st Lt. Arthur Hitchcock joined the 25th USCT's Company D. He had been promoted to second lieutenant from private of the 3rd Regiment Veteran Reserve Corps. The 25th saw action in North Carolina, Louisiana, and Florida. He was mustered out with the company on December 6, 1865. (U.S. Army Military History Institute.)

Surgeon Thomas Howley of the 25th USCT joined the regiment in January 1864. He likely used his medical training after the troops saw action in Louisiana and Florida. Howley was mustered out with the regiment on December 6, 1865. (U.S. Army Military History Institute.)

Capt. John W. Migrath was mustered in on January 25, 1864, and led the 25th USCT's Company B. Although Migrath likely received training at the military school for white officers in Philadelphia, 1210 Chestnut Street, military records indicate that he was dismissed from the army for an undisclosed reason on November 22, 1864. (U.S. Army Military History Institute.)

The facial image of Ed Hamilton's *Spirit of Freedom* is engraved at the top of his moving sculpture in Washington's Shaw district. That spirit is what often drove the black soldiers, including those from Camp William Penn, to endure horrific conditions and battles in order to persevere. (Donald Scott Sr.)

On April 26, 1864, 2nd Lt. John E. Norcross was mustered in and joined the 25th USCT. Although he obtained the rank of brevet captain on June 20, 1865, he was dismissed on that date by special order. (U.S. Army Military History Institute.)

Capt. Eliphelet B. Norris was mustered in on August 13, 1862, and joined the 25th USCT. He had been promoted from first sergeant of the 126th Regiment New York Volunteers to second lieutenant on February 10, 1864, before rising to the rank of adjutant on March 22, 1864. He achieved the rank of captain on April 18, 1865, after he and his regiment saw action in North Carolina, Louisiana, and Florida. He was mustered out with the company on December 6, 1865. (U.S. Army Military History Institute.)

Capt. William A. Prickett was first mustered in on August 9, 1862. Prickett was promoted from sergeant of the 14th Regiment New Jersey Volunteers on February 4, 1864. He most likely trained at the Free Military School for Applicants to Command Colored Troops in Philadelphia, joining Company G of the 25th USCT. Prickett mustered out with his regiment on December 6, 1865. (U.S. Army Military History Institute.)

These are likely soldiers of Camp William Penn, according to bibliographic material at the Library Company of Philadelphia where the photograph was found. Although their regiment has not been identified, several of the black soldiers are standing with an officer or someone with a managerial role. (Library Company of Philadelphia.)

Lt. Col. J. W. H. Reisinger was originally mustered in on September 4, 1862. Reisinger was promoted from captain of Company H, 150th Regiment Pennsylvania Volunteers, to major on March 12, 1864. He was promoted to lieutenant colonel on November 16, 1864. He probably trained at the Free Military School for Applicants to Command Colored Troops in Philadelphia, joining the 25th Regiment USCT. Reisinger mustered out with his regiment on December 6, 1865. (U.S. Army Military History Institute.)

Capt. Jasper H. Warren was first mustered in on September 18, 1862. Warren was promoted from sergeant of Company A of the 13th Regiment New Hampshire Volunteers on March 3, 1864. He joined the 25th USCT Company I. He likely trained at the military school for white officers in Philadelphia at 1210 Chestnut Street. Warren mustered out with his regiment on December 6, 1865. (U.S. Army Military History Institute.)

Capt. William B. Wright was originally mustered in on June 2, 1861. He was promoted from sergeant of Company H, 26th Regiment Pennsylvania Volunteers, on January 26, 1864. Wright joined Company C of the 25th Regiment USCT. He probably trained at a military school for white officers in Philadelphia. (U.S. Army Military History Institute.)

Assistant surgeon Charles J. Adams was first mustered in on March 31, 1864. He was promoted from hospital steward of the 13th U.S. Infantry on March 31, 1864, joining the 25th USCT. Adams most likely trained at the Free Military School for Applicants to Command Colored Troops in Philadelphia. He mustered out with his regiment on December 6, 1865. (U.S. Army Military History Institute.)

Capt. Charles E. Brigham was originally mustered in on February 6, 1864. He was promoted from first lieutenant on May 11, 1865, joining Company D of the 25th Regiment USCT. Brigham likely trained at the military school for white officers in Philadelphia at 1210 Chestnut Street. He mustered out with his regiment on December 6, 1865. (U.S. Army Military History Institute.)

Capt. Charles W. Green was first mustered in on August 18, 1862. He was promoted from private of Company B, 13th Regiment New Hampshire Volunteers. He joined Company E of the 25th Regiment USCT. He most likely trained at the Free Military School for Applicants to Command Colored Troops in Philadelphia. Green mustered out with his regiment on December 6, 1865. (U.S. Army Military History Institute.)

This image of "the Colored Volunteer Marching into Dixie" and published by Currier and Ives of New York was very encouraging for blacks seeking to enroll at such places as Camp William Penn. Many of the ex-slaves relished the thought of returning back to areas of enslavement to free loved ones and for justice. (Library Company of Philadelphia.)

March 8, 1864, was the date that 1st Lt. Nathan L. Gano was originally mustered in. Gano was promoted from sergeant of the 121st Regiment New York Volunteers, joining Company H of the 25th Regiment USCT. Gano mustered out with his regiment on December 6, 1865. (U.S. Army Military History Institute.)

Pvt. William C. Baxter served with Company A of the 25th USCT from Camp William Penn. He was likely at the camp when the regiment was organized between June 13 and August 19, 1864, and served in several major Virginia battles before being mustered out in Brownsville, Texas, on November 4, 1865. (U.S. Army Military History Institute.)

Capt. Chester A. Greenleaf was mustered into the 25th USCT's Company F on February 3, 1864. Greenleaf, similar to other white officers of his rank, was likely trained at the Free Military School for Applicants to Command Colored Troops, based at 1210 Chestnut Street in Philadelphia. Greenleaf and the regiment were mustered out in December 1865. (U.S. Army Military History Institute.)

Quartermaster James M. Dudley mustered into service on January 26, 1864, when he joined the 25th Regiment USCT at Camp William Penn. He mustered out of the regiment on December 6, 1865. (U.S. Army Military History Institute.)

Attacking the last line of rebels blocking the way to Petersburg, the 22nd USCT from Camp William Penn was featured in the July 9, 1864, edition of *Frank Leslie's Illustrated Newspaper* as part of Duncan's Brigade. The sketch by the paper's "special artist" Edwin Forbes captures the fierceness of the unit in the background as a black corporal confers with his captain while others carry one of their wounded comrades away. (Library of Congress.)

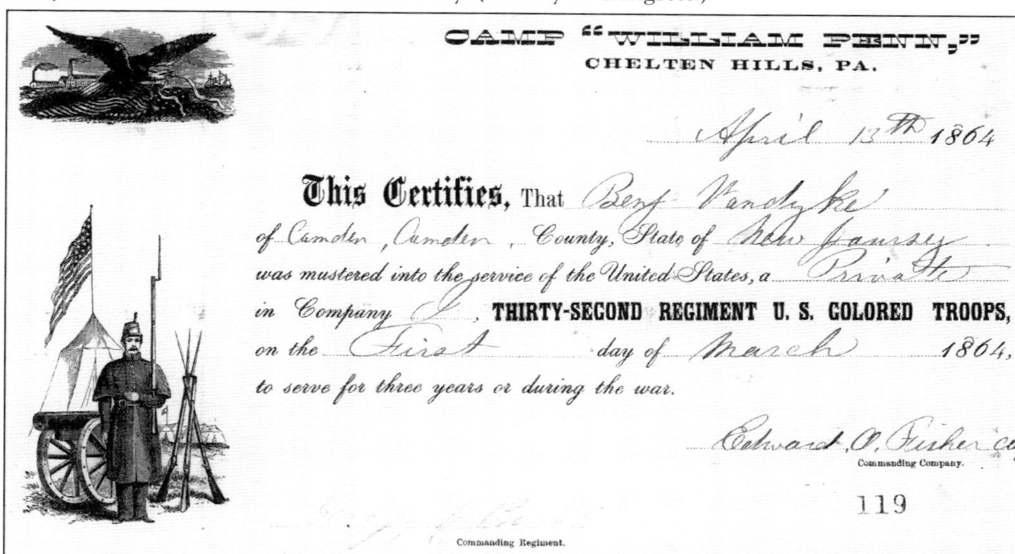

CAMP "WILLIAM PENN,"
CHELTEN HILLS, PA.

April 13th 1864

This Certifies, That Benj Vandyke
of Camden, Camden, County, State of New Jersey
was mustered into the service of the United States, a Private
in Company I, THIRTY-SECOND REGIMENT U. S. COLORED TROOPS,
on the First day of March 1864,
to serve for three years or during the war.

Edward O. Fisher Cap
Commanding Company.

119

Commanding Regiment.

Discharged Aug 22, 1865

Benjamin Vandyke joined the 32nd Regiment's Company K as a private on March 1, 1864. Signed by Capt. Edward Fisher, a handwritten note at the bottom of the document indicates he was discharged on August 22, 1865. Just before mustering out with the rest of the 32nd, Vandyke likely served garrison duty at Charleston, Beaufort, and Hilton Head in South Carolina. (New Jersey State Archives.)

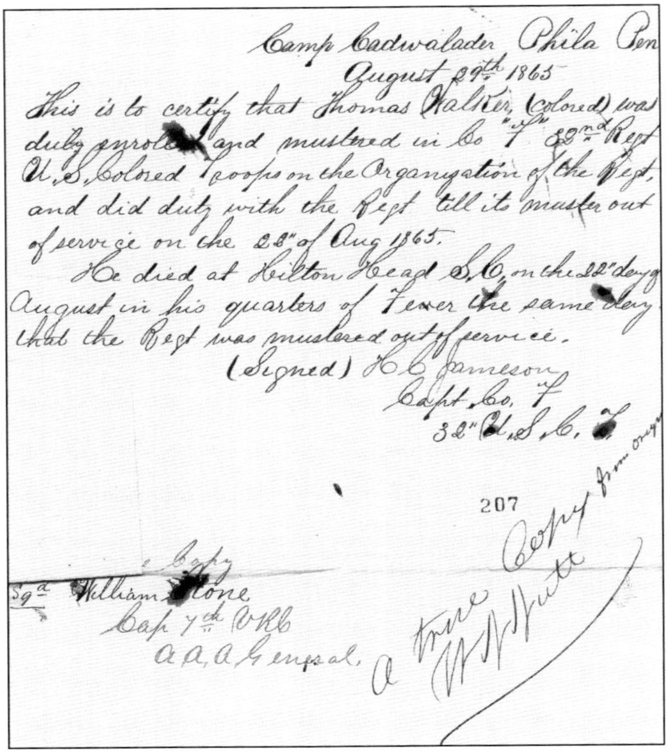

Camp Cadwalader Phila Pen
August 29th 1865

This is to certify that Thomas Walker, (colored) was duly enrolled and mustered in Co "F" 32nd Regt U.S. Colored Troops on the Organization of the Regt, and did duty with the Regt till its muster out of service on the 22d of Aug 1865.

He died at Hilton Head S.C. on the 22d day of August in his quarters of Fever the same day that the Regt was mustered out of service.

(Signed) H.C. Jameson
Capt. Co. F
32d U.S.C.T.

207

Copy
Sgd William Stone
Cap 7th VRC
A.A.A General.

A true Copy from original
[illegible]

Thomas Walker died of "fever" in Hilton Head, South Carolina, on the very day his 32nd Regiment was mustered out of service on August 22, 1865, according to this letter. Walker, a Camden, New Jersey, resident, apparently had a wife who needed his state funds. Nearly 115 of the regiment's men died by disease, say military records. (New Jersey State Archives.)

Sgt. Alexander Smothers mustered into service on February 24, 1864, and joined Company F of the 32nd USCT Regiment at Camp William Penn. He was promoted to sergeant major on September 1, 1864. (U.S. Army Military History Institute.)

Pvt. Gabriel Butler, a soldier in the 43rd USCT of Camp William Penn, is shown following the war in Monessen, around 1912–1914. The 43rd was the first black regiment to participate in a U.S. presidential inauguration in March 1865 after Abraham Lincoln took office for a second time. The regiment participated in some of the fiercest fighting of the facility's brigades. (Lee Carol Cook.)

Posing for the camera are 2nd Lt. Richard C. Phillips of the 43rd USCT and his wife, Roda. Although such photographs are relatively rare, some have turned up in the files of historical repositories and private collections. (U.S. Army Military History Institute.)

Surgeon Al Waterhouse was mustered into service on July 24, 1862, and became assistant surgeon of the 7th Regular Maine Volunteers. He was promoted to surgeon on March 17, 1864, and served the 43rd USCT of Camp William Penn. The 43rd saw action as part of the Army of the Potomac with some companies participating in the bloody Battle of the Crater in Virginia on July 30, 1864, suffering heavy losses. (U.S. Army Military History Institute.)

Citizens Volunteer Hospital was not far from the eateries and saloons near the waterfront that served recruits and officers, including many from Camp William Penn, before they went to war. Located at Broad Street and Washington Avenue, the hospital's exterior is bustling with activity, including the escorting and carrying of the wounded to the facility. (Free Library of Philadelphia.)

Christian Morris, who served in the 43rd USCT, had a strong gaze that reflected his advanced age, sagaciousness, and war experiences. In addition to being injured, he suffered from scurvy and rheumatic fever. However, he lived a long life to about age 75, after marrying Susan Williams on April 2, 1863. The couple had 13 children, including five or six who survived to adulthood. One son, Rev. Joseph Edward Morris, born on November 24, 1866, in Highville, Lancaster County, became an AME preacher and trustee of the black AME college, Wilberforce. Christian Morris died on February 19, 1913, of a cerebral hemorrhage at the Soldiers and Sailors Home in Erie, where he is buried in the veterans' cemetery. (Lee Carol Cook.)

The 45th USCT's flag, designed by David Bustill Bowser, features a black soldier holding the American flag with a bust of Pres. George Washington in the background. Bowser's ancestor, Cyrus Bustill reportedly risked his life to deliver bread to Washington's troops at Valley Forge during the Revolutionary War. According to historian Charles L. Blockson, Bustill was the great-great-great-grandfather of Paul L. Robeson, a renowned black scholar, lawyer, athlete, and entertainer. (Library of Congress.)

Capt. Jacob Ormerod led Company K of the 45th USCT. That regiment had been active as the war culminated, participating in such Virginia battles as Fair Oaks and the Appomattox campaign. (U.S. Army Military History Institute.)

On April 20, 1864, 1st Lt. Edwin Walton Jr. was mustered in. He joined Company C of the 45th USCT at Camp William Penn and likely saw action in Virginia, including at the Battle of New Market Heights or Chaffin's Farm in September 1864. He was mustered out with his company on November 4, 1865, after frontier duty at Brownsville, Texas. (U.S. Army Military History Institute.)

The black soldier marches off to war as Lady Liberty is depicted on the flag of the 127th USCT, designed by David Bustill Bowser. The soldiers fought with an inspiring motto: "We will prove ourselves men." In the background is likely a depiction of Camp William Penn that consisted early on of a sparkling expanse of white tents in the rolling hills of Chelten Hills. (Library of Congress.)

Sgt. Samuel Wright, an African American who achieved rank, mustered into service on August 29, 1864, and joined the 127th Regiment USCT at Camp William Penn. However, blacks were systematically blocked from reaching higher ranks during this time. In this postwar photograph, he is likely a member of a chapter of the GAR. (U.S. Army Military History Institute.)

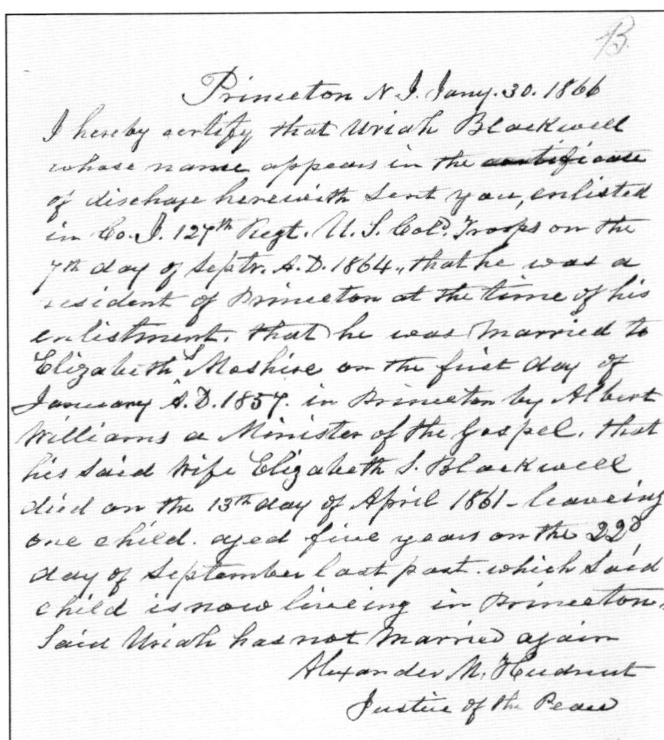

B

Princeton N.J. Jany. 30. 1866

I hereby certify that Uriah Blackwell whose name appears in the certificate of discharge herewith sent you, enlisted in Co. I. 127th Regt. U.S. Col. Troops on the 7th day of Septr. A.D. 1864, that he was a resident of Princeton at the time of his enlistment, that he was married to Elizabeth S. Moshire on the first day of January A.D. 1857. in Princeton by Albert Williams a Minister of the Gospel. that his said wife Elizabeth S. Blackwell died on the 13th day of April 1861 - leaving one child. aged five years on the 22d day of September last past. which said child is now living in Princeton. Said Uriah has not married again

Alexander M. Hudnut
Justice of the Peace

29

Uriah Blackwell, a private in Company I of the 127th USCT, received a letter of support from a justice of the peace of Princeton, New Jersey, to obtain financial assistance following the war. Blackwell apparently married with the blessings of "a Minister of the Gospel" his wife Elizabeth well before the war. Although Elizabeth died at the start of the war on April 13, 1861, she and her husband had one child whom Blackwell was responsible for, according to the letter. Furthermore, he had not remarried, but had to fight for financial support, despite mustering in on September 7, 1864, and likely marching with his regiment to City Point, Virginia, later in the month. (New Jersey State Archives.)

Capt. Edward N. Williard mustered into service on September 14, 1864, joining Company C of the 127th Regiment USCT at Camp William Penn. He transferred to Company B. He mustered out of company on October 20, 1865. (U.S. Army Military History Institute.)

Williard appears to be quite comfortable in the years following the war. As a member of the GAR, he likely fraternized with other Camp William Penn warriors of the past. (U.S. Army Military History Institute.)

Some Camp William Penn soldiers joined the famed Buffalo soldier units following the Civil War. Many of the troops were assigned to the Texas Rio Grande following the war and likely became instrumental in commemorating Juneteenth, marking the end of slavery in Texas. (U.S. Army Military History Institute.)

As commander of all U.S. troops during the Civil War and destined to become an American president, Ulysses S. Grant was friends with Jay Cooke, the "financier of the Civil War." Following the war, Grant would visit the Cooke estate and the Chelten Hills area because his son Jesse attended a local military academy. Grant, as commander of all U.S. forces during the war, was naturally in charge of the black regiments at Camp William Penn during the later years of the great struggle. Women's rights advocate and antislavery freedom fighter Lucretia Mott visited the two men at Cooke's nearby Ogontz estate following the war to stop the hanging of Native American leaders in the far west. (Library of Congress.)

Gen. Benjamin Butler commissioned Anthony C. Paquet to design a special medal to be given to 300 USCT troops in appreciation for battles fought at Fort Harrison and Fort Gilmer under his command in 1864. The Tiffany silver medals displayed heroism but carried no official status and were imprinted with "Army of the James . . . Distinguished for courage Campaign before Richmond 1864 . . . Ferro lis Libertas Preniet," and "U.S. Colored Troops." The troops were forbidden to wear the medals on their lapels after Butler was relieved of his command. (Picture Collection, the Branch Libraries, the New York Public Library; Astor, Lenox, and Tilden Foundations.)

The former Union general Benjamin F. Butler (sitting left) is shown as a member of the U.S. House of Representatives. Rep. Thaddeus Stevens of Lancaster, whose name appeared on recruitment posters for black soldiers, is seated adjacent to him in this 1868 photograph. Butler and Stevens were very early proponents of recruiting black troops and supported the establishment of Camp William Penn. A medallion bearing Butler's name was given to valiant black soldiers during the war. Butler eventually became governor of Massachusetts in 1882, although he unsuccessfully ran for U.S. president in 1884. (Library of Congress.)

Three

TRUTH MARCHES ON

Frederick Douglass, the most renowned antislavery abolitionist of his time, spoke to the men of the 3rd Regiment USCT at Camp William Penn in late July 1863. He was born a slave in February 1818 as Frederick Augustus Washington Bailey near Easton, Maryland, and his mother, Harriet Bailey, was also a slave. His father was an unidentified white man. After escaping North as a young man with the help of such abolitionists as Edward M. Davis—Lucretia Mott's son-in-law who was instrumental in the establishment of Camp William Penn—Douglass became a prolific speaker after years of self-educating. His gift for speaking was realized by such abolitionist greats as William Lloyd Garrison and Lucretia Mott. Douglass became a well-known antislavery lecturer in America and England where he temporarily fled slave catchers to raise money for his freedom. As years passed, Douglass became a prolific newspaper editor and started his own publication, the *North Star.* A paid army recruiter, Douglass's two sons joined the Union army with one fighting for the Massachusetts 54th black regiment on South Carolina's Morris Island about the time he spoke to the soldiers of Camp William Penn. (Library of Congress.)

William Bowser (1842–1945) was one of the first black settlers in the Camptown or LaMott area. He arrived after the Civil War in 1869, when Lucretia Mott's son-in-law Edward M. Davis subdivided the property in the area via his land-development firm. Davis's other clients included rich tycoons such as banker Jay Cooke. (Perry Triplett and Citizens for the Restoration of Historic LaMott.)

This, the oldest house standing in LaMott, was the home of William Butcher, the first black to settle in the area in 1850 when the Fugitive Slave Act was passed. The law, which set the North and South on a collision course, allowed slave catchers to re-enslave blacks in virtually every area of the country. Many runaway slaves sought refuge in LaMott, previously known as Camptown, with the likes of Lucretia Mott and Edward M. Davis, who employed Butcher as a tenant farmer. The house sits at the southeast corner of Willow Avenue and Butcher Street. (Norman Triplett and Old York Road Historical Society.)

The original LaMott fire station on Willow Avenue began serving the local community in 1910. Although the station moved several blocks away to a more modern facility, the Willow Avenue location had been used as a museum to house important artifacts of Camp William Penn via Citizens for the Historic Restoration of LaMott. The group is now upgrading its facility with future plans calling for the construction of a new museum and other facilities related to Camp William Penn. (Norman Triplett and Old York Road Historical Society.)

This early-1900s photograph shows children who attended the local school at Sycamore and Willow Avenues, which became the LaMott Community Center. Lucretia Mott's son-in-law Edward M. Davis, according to the Old York Road Historical Society, constructed the first school in the area then known as Camptown in 1868, just several years after the Civil War. The integrated student body reveals the early progressiveness of the area, established by such early local Quakers as the Motts. (Norman Triplett and Old York Road Historical Society.)

This photograph shows the front gate and main entrance of Camp William Penn with the state historic marker. A refurbishing of the original gate was financed by various sponsors via a local community group, Citizens for the Restoration of Historic LaMott, headed by LaMott community activist Perry Triplett. The group today is carrying on Triplett's dream of establishing a new museum and other facilities in the neighborhood of LaMott, named after the Quaker women's rights advocate and antislavery abolitionist. (Donald Scott Jr.)

The LaMott AME Church rises in the background as a plaque commemorates the great historic richness of the community where Camp William Penn once stood. Situated on Cheltenham Avenue near Broad Street, the sign and church are very visible from the busy highway. The house to the right was once church property, with all of the land previously a part of the sprawling 13-acre facility. (Kristopher Scott.)

Thomas I. Dawson of Philadelphia harbors the medal of his grandfather Prestley Dorsey. Although the inscription reads: "P. Dorsey; Co. H; 43rd Pa. Vol. Inf.," Dorsey actually served in Company H of the 43rd USCT from Camp William Penn. His unit participated in such Virginia battles as Hatcher's Run, the Rapidan campaign, and the Mine Explosion Assault at Petersburg. Ironically, today Dawson lives across the street from where the camp once stood. (Donald Scott Sr.)

Civil War reenactors of the 3rd Regiment USCT Infantry march in Washington, D.C., during the dedication of the African American Civil War Memorial in 1999. Most of the men in the unit are from the Philadelphia area and routinely contribute to history programs throughout the United States. (Donald Scott Sr.)

This state plaque of the Pennsylvania Historical and Museum Commission commemorates the spot where Lucretia Mott's home once stood. Adjacent to Camp William Penn, it was an epicenter of the Underground Railroad and attracted the top abolitionists of the time, including orator Frederick Douglass, supreme conductor Harriet Tubman, and William Still, the "Father of the Underground Railroad." The style of the home that can be partially seen to the left resembles Mott's residence where she moved to in 1857. (Donald Scott Jr.)

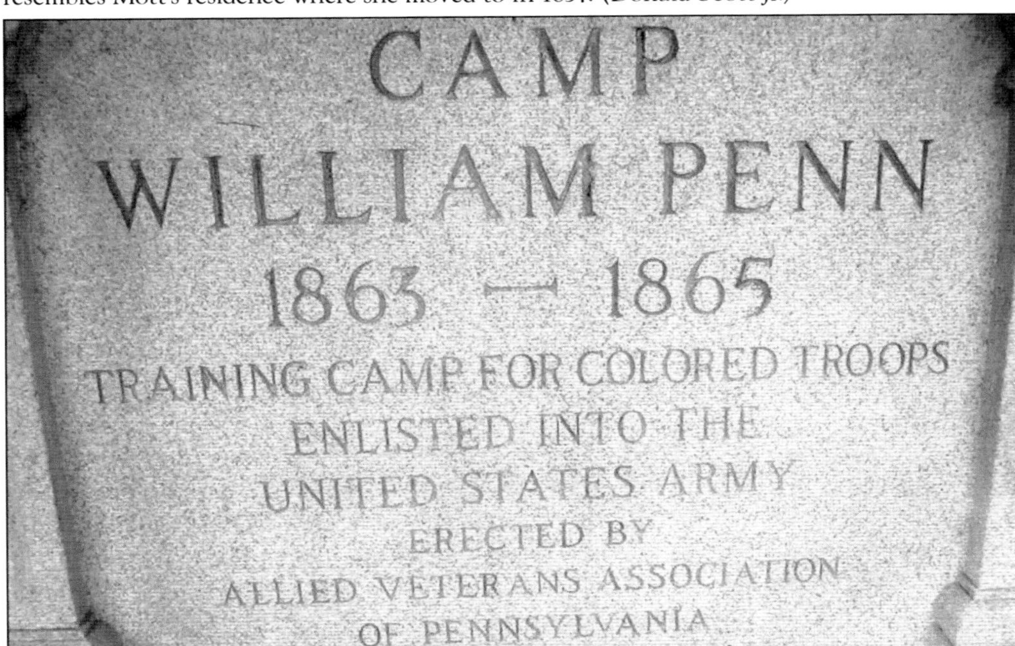

This historic marker at the intersection of Willow Avenue and Sycamore Avenue in LaMott has graced the neighborhood for more than 65 years. It is often the centerpiece of local parades, celebrating July 4, Memorial Day, Veteran's Day, and Juneteenth, which commemorates black emancipation in Texas where many of the Camp William Penn soldiers were discharged at the end of the war. (Donald Scott Jr.)

BIBLIOGRAPHY

Bacon, Margret Hope. *Valiant Friend: The Life of Lucretia Mott*. New York: Walker and Company, 1980.

Bates, Samuel P. *History of the Pennsylvania Volunteers, 1861-5*. Wilmington, NC: Broadfoot, 1993.

Blockson, Charles L. *African Americans in Pennsylvania Above Ground and Underground: An Illustrated Guide*. Harrisburg, PA: RB Books, 2001.

Claxton, Melvin, and Mark Puls. *Uncommon Valor: A Story of Race, Patriotism, and Glory in the Final Battles of the Civil War*. Hoboken, NJ: John Wiley and Sons, 2006.

Gates, Henry Louis Jr., and Evelyn Brooks Higginbotham. *African American Lives*. New York: Oxford University Press, 2004.

Gladstone, William A. *Men of Color*. Gettysburg, PA: Thomas Publications, 1993.

Handler, Jerome S., and Michael L. Tuite Jr. "Retouching History: The Modern Falsification of a Civil War Photograph." http://people.virginia.edu/~jh3v/retouchinghistory/essay.html.

Paradis, James M. *African Americans and the Gettysburg Campaign*. Lanham, MD: the Scarecrow Press, 2005.

———. "Strike the Blow: A Study of the Sixth Regiment of the United States Colored Infantry." PhD diss., Temple University, 1995.

Scott, Donald. "Camp William Penn's Black Soldiers in Blue." Leesburg, VA: *America's Civil War*, November, 1999.

Shaffer, Donald R. *After the Glory: The Struggles of Black Civil War Veterans*. Lawrence, KS: University Press of Kansas, 2004.

Smith, Eric L., and Joe W. Trotter. *African Americans in Pennsylvania: Shifting Historical Perspectives*. State College, PA: Pennsylvania State University Press, 1997.

Trudeau, Noah Andre. *Like Men of War: Black Troops in the Civil War 1862–1865*. Boston: Little, Brown and Company, 1998.